CHRISTIAN SOLDIERS!
DON'T DESERT THE FIELD!

Dr. Jerry Terrebrood

Paperback-Press
an imprint of A & S Publishing
A & S Holmes, Inc.

ISBN-13: 978-0692706695
ISBN-10: 0692706690

CONTENTS

DEDICATION

This book is dedicated to all of those persons throughout history who have given their lives for the sake of the Gospel; many gave much of their lives and many gave their life unto the death.

America was founded upon the principles of religious freedom; despite what revisionists would falsely claim. The founder's motives for coming to America are being impugned daily as myth and fable at all levels in this once great country.

Among the many profound statements made by the late President Ronald Reagan, none speak to me more than this:

"Without God, there is no virtue, because there's no prompting of the conscience. Without God, we're mired in the material, that flat world that tells us only what the senses perceive. Without God, there is a coarsening of the society. And without God, democracy will not and cannot long endure. If we ever forget that we're one nation under God, then we will be a nation gone under."

We face some sobering facts in this country: (a) Freedom is not free; it is always bought and paid for by blood, sweat, and tears, (b) Religious freedom is only guaranteed by those willing to buy it with the same commodities.

Dr. Jerry Terrebrood

Part I

Socialism and Secular Humanism

Proverbs 14:1
"The fool says in his heart, 'There is no God.'"

Whatever happened to the "good old USA?" For those of us born and raised in the real era of "Happy Days" it is nauseating just to read the news. What began so nobly as a Christian Nation has been turned upside down. That which was moral, good, and right has become the enemy of the institutional system. That which was only spoken of in whispers and privately, has become glaring and brazen fodder for nearly all of the media. Those for which God destroyed Sodom and Gomorrah have become one of the most vocal, protected, and forceful entities in the formation of our laws and customs in this once "greatest nation in the world!" Those actions which God's Word calls an abomination have become that which society claims is right and acceptable in our nation and most of the world.

How? Why? What happened?

Socialism came to America in a clandestine and evil form in the early 1930s.

SOCIALISM:

"On August 4, 1914, the Social Democrats stood in the Reichstag and, to a man, voted the Kaiser's war credits, joining the orgy of patriotism as the armies of the Reich smashed into Belgium. Marxists were stunned. The long anticipated European war was to be their time. Marx had thundered in the closing line of his *Communist Manifesto,* "Workers of the world, unite!" Marxists had confidently predicted that when war came, the workers would rise up and rebel against their rulers rather than fight fellow workers of neighboring nations. But it had not happened. The greatest socialist party in Europe had been converted into a war party, and the workers had thrown down their tools and gone off to fight with songs in their hearts...Marxists had been exposed as fools...

Trotsky sought to make the Red Army the spear point of revolution. Invading Poland, he was hurled back at the Vistula by Polish patriots under Marshal Pilsudski. Nothing the Marxists had predicted had come to pass. Their hour had come and gone. The workers of the west, the mythical proletariat, had refused to play the role history had assigned them. How could Marx have been so wrong?

Two of Marx's disciples now advanced an explanation. Yes, Marx had been wrong. Capitalism was not impoverishing the workers. Indeed, their lot was improving, and they had not risen in revolution because their souls had been saturated in two thousand years of Christianity, which blinded them to their true class interests. Unless and until Christianity and Western culture…were uprooted from the soul of Western Man, Marxism could not take root…In biblical terms, the word of Marx, seed of the revolution, had fallen on rock-hard Christian soil and died. Wagering everything on the working class, the Marxists had bet on the wrong horse…

The first dissenting disciple was the Hungarian Georg Lukacs…(recognized as) a Marxist theorist to rival Marx himself. 'I saw the revolutionary destruction of society as the one and only solution,' said Lukacs. 'A worldwide overturning of values cannot take place without the annihilation of the old values and the creation of new ones by the revolutionaries.'… Lukacs put his self-described 'demonic' ideas into action in what came to be known as 'cultural terrorism.'

As part of this terrorism he instituted a radical sex education program in Hungarian schools. Children were instructed in free love, sexual intercourse, the archaic nature of middle-class family codes, the outdatedness of monogamy, and the irrelevance of religions, which deprives man of all pleasures. Women too, were called to rebel against the sexual mores of the time...Five decades after Lukacs fled Hungary, his ideas would be enthusiastically embraced by (America's) baby boomers in the 'sexual revolution.'

The second disciple was Antonio Gramsci, an Italian Communist who has lately begun to receive deserved recognition as the greatest Marxist strategist of the twentieth century...

Rather than seize power first and impose a cultural revolution from above, Gramsci argued, Marxists in the West must first change the culture; then power would fall into their laps like ripened fruit. But, to change the culture would require a 'long march through the institutions'—the arts, cinema, theater, schools, colleges, seminaries, newspapers, magazines, and the new electronic medium, (in his day) radio. One by one, each had to be captured and converted and politicized into an agency of revolution. Then the people could be slowly educated to understand and even welcome the revolution...

To the new Marxist, the path to power was nonviolent and would require decades of patient labor. Victory would come only after Christian beliefs had died in the soul of Western Man...

With the assistance of Columbia University, (in 1933) they (European Marxists from the Frankfurt University in Berlin) set up their new Frankfurt School in New York City and redirected their talents and energies to undermining the culture of the country that had given them refuge (from the Nazis in Germany).

Among the new weapons of cultural conflict the Frankfurt School developed was Critical Theory. The name sounds benign enough, but it stands for a practice that is anything but benign. One student of Critical theory defined it as the 'essentially destructive criticism of all the main elements of western culture, including Christianity, capitalism, authority, the family, patriarchy, hierarchy, morality, tradition, sexual restraint, loyalty, patriotism, nationalism, heredity, ethnocentrism, convention and conservatism.'

Using Critical Theory, for example, the cultural Marxist repeats and repeats the charge that the West is guilty of genocidal crimes against every civilization and culture it has encountered. Under Critical Theory, one repeats and repeats that Western societies are history's greatest repositories of racism, sexism, nativism, xenophobia, homophobia, anti-Semitism, fascism, and Nazism. Under Critical Theory, the crimes of the West flow from the character of the West as shaped by Christianity. One modern example is 'attack politics,' where 'surrogates' and 'spin doctors' never defend their own candidate, but attack and attack the opposition." Patrick J. Buchanan; *The Death of the West* (comments in parentheses are mine).

The Critical Theory advance, discussed in the foregoing, is based upon the belief, and the proven results, that if you never answer the oppositions questions or challenges, but find some area where you can accuse them, and if you repeat the accusations often enough and long enough, society will come to believe it, then you never have to worry about the questions of the opposition.

At this point one should consider current terms such as "Political Correctness" which accuses anyone differing with the government of being prejudiced, a racist, a hate monger, etc.

Also consider the new name given to the Socialist cause: "Progressives."

We wonder how this happened, when it happened, and why it happened. We need only to look at the platform of the Democratic left, beginning with George McGovern, and culminating in Barak Obama, who was reared and succored by socialists--and that is a fact--and who demonstrates by his actions that he is a socialist and apparently still a closet Muslim.

Having read the foregoing, does "change America fundamentally" now have a slightly different ring to it?

Currently we have Hillary Clinton trying to climb to the forefront. She demonstrates by her statements, history and actions that she is a "far left" socialist supporter of LBGT and that she cannot be trusted to tell the truth.

SECULAR HUMANISM:

Perhaps the world, in times past, has been more wicked than it currently is. But, this treatise concerns itself primarily with the United States; a nation that was founded upon religious freedom by religious people. It was intended to have a government of the people, by the people, and for the people. But, the people have strayed far afield from the founding father's noble beginnings.

In fairness, a brief glance, at the long history of the Christian religion, shows significant evidence, that during certain eras the Church was infected with corruption, greed, and the lust for power. Is it then any wonder that men and women began to doubt the righteousness of the religious elite and the veracity of the claims they made about a compassionate savior?

At times, the Church has been its own worst enemy: partially because of the sanctimonious nature of what had, in many cases, become the state religion. And partially, because of a growing secularism that appealed to man's own self-serving nature that strives to be independent of any outside agency that would try to prescribe what is moral or immoral, right or wrong, acceptable or unacceptable, in thought and practice.

Man treasures the idea that each individual shapes his own destiny. Religion has often been thought of as a contrived "boogey man in the sky" concept, with which to keep society under some measure of control.

Society has, of necessity, maintained some form of laws and rules that limit the exercise of an individual's freedom toward the freedoms of a neighboring individual. However, an orderly society dare not prize the rights and freedoms of the individual above the rights of the populace—case in point: the Roman Empire.

Therefore, society requires established moral law and order. The public would have no rights to life, property, freedom, religion, etc., if a neighbor were free to take any of those away.

Of course where there are laws and regulation, there are always those in power, or those seeking power, who will twist and distort the law to suit and support their own agenda.

The questions then become:

(a) Does law and order come from the conscience and good will of the people? (b) Is it a divinely implanted sense of right and wrong with which we are born? (c) Was the sense of Law set forth from human experience, or inherently made known to man by a righteous God?

The secular humanists ask: "God? What God?" The arrogance of man, and the refusal to believe in any power greater than self, forces the asking of that question. That question leads to others: What is morality? What is legal? Why can't I do what I want to do when I want to do it if I believe it is right for me?

When the assumption has been made, that there is no such person as God, man is left with a plethora of unanswerable questions. If there is no God: How did we get here? How did the earth happen? What keeps the Sun, the Moon, the Earth, all properly aligned, etc.?

There is a story of an atheist who went to court seeking a National Atheist Day. His case was predicated on the facts that the nation has Christmas, President's Day, *Channukah,* Independence Day, etc. After the judge listened to his case, the judge stated, "You already have a National Atheists Day." The man contested the judges statement with a question, "What day would that be?" The judge replied, "Why April 1st, "the fool has said in his heart, 'there is no God,'" quoting Proverbs 14:1.

In man's attempt to answer these questions of life, without acknowledging a God of intricate design and power, our children are taught in school, as truth, the natural and random evolution of species through adaptation and mutation, and, the random incidental development of planets over millions/billions of years. This of course is inspired by, and fits perfectly, the socialist plans previously described.

Students are pointed to a fabricated chart of a non-existent record of fossil progressions. Thus, they often come to believe that they are nothing special; they are not created as individuals by the infinite workings of Almighty God. They are just the result of the accidental formation of a "gob of goo" that mutated itself into human beings, over millions and perhaps billions of years.

What answers do the children receive in the church as refutation? "The Bible says!" That is true. And, for some, that may be sufficient. But, if we truly examine who is attending the churches and who is not and the results of "youth flight," it may provide a very sharp focus on the inadequacy of that approach.

Many clergymen are unable to provide meaningful information as proof that the Bible is true concerning creation and that the atheistic theory of evolution is unproven. They may believe this to be true, but their only defense is the Scripture itself. Our students are taught that the Bible is nothing but myths and superstitions.

Since the humanist philosophy, in the humanist mind, rules out the veracity of Scripture in the process of teaching evolution, Scripture is not acceptable evidence to the teenager in public school. When the student confronts church teaching with, "My teacher said," what else do ministers know, that can effectively answer a student's inquiry?

For very mature Christians, the pastor's stand upon the Word is sufficient—while many of the young people go out the door and do not come back.

Today, there are many excellent and scientific sources that provide tremendously important arguments against the theory of evolution and positive scientific support for creation.

Evolutional theory, in my opinion, is the heart that beats within the body of Socialism. Since no one alive was there when God created, as described in Genesis, it is an event obviously unobservable, unpredictable, and unrepeatable. Those are the three main requirements that scientists insist upon in order to declare something factual. It is called the rules of "empirical evidence."

For instance, gravity cannot be seen. But the results of gravity are observable, predictable, and repeatable. Therefore, scientifically, gravity is a fact.

What is displayed in museums as evidence of the evolutionary process is most often extreme supposition based upon very scant, if any, real evidence. Yet, it is displayed as fact.

One of the most effective weapons against the evolutional theory of mutation from a lower state, to a higher state, comes from the observance of "irreducible complexity." The term just stated means that some organisms are so uniquely organized, with so many absolutely essential elements, that the absence of just one would render it totally inoperative. Therefore, how could it have evolved over millions or billions of years, if it were totally non-functional, and therefore totally useless, until all of the uniquely formed and properly joined components were present?

These terms and thought processes will be examined in greater detail in later chapters.

Sadly, there are those in the Christian Church who have begun to accept the notion that God was the initial cause, but evolution was the process by which He created. This is coined as "Theistic Evolution." I suspect this compromise is an effort to gain some level of worldly acceptance, or a blatant inability to respond intellectually.

The Army of God must equip itself, through education, to boldly practice logical apologetics in the face of scientists whom the secular world holds to be an infallible source of truth. However, we have seen down through history in the United States, and throughout the world, that scientists have had to change their views on many issues once thought to be fact.

Although there may be some minor verbiage disagreements among scholars concerning textual variances, the central truth of the Bible has stood the test of time, and more and more evidence is gathered annually that supports the truth it contains.

Many would argue: The Bible says it. I believe it. That settles it. To which I would respond that it may settle it for some, but for others, who are faced with questions being generated by the secular influences they encounter, they need more information than that position provides.

Like many clergymen, many parents are ill equipped to respond with credible answers for their children who are being told by the public school system that religion is myth and there is no God. The children have yet to recognize the significantly greater amount of faith it takes to believe in the unproven theory of Evolution than to have faith in God who proves Himself in so many different ways in the lives of the believers. They are simply told to "learn" from the public purveyors of information.

If one were to examine the fossil record, as illustrated in the average high school biology book, and stack all of the intermediate fossil stages that Darwinism supposes to have existed, from trilobites to man, one on top of the other, many scientists have remarked that the fossil record would be about 2 ½ miles deep--whereas the actual fossil record vanishes from the depths of the earth at about 200 feet.

"Charles Darwin had a problem—a huge one. He couldn't name any transitional forms in his *Origin of Species* (1859). Instead he devoted a whole chapter to lamenting "The Imperfection of the Geological Record," in which he wrote: 'Geology assuredly does not reveal any such finely graduated organic chain; and this, perhaps, is the most obvious and gravest objection which can be urged against my theory. The explanation lies, as I believe, in the extreme imperfection of the geological record.'

Darwin didn't have this problem by himself. Dr. Colin Patterson (1933-1998), senior Paleontologist at the British Museum of natural History, London, when asked why he had no illustrations of evolutionary transitions in his 1978 book *Evolution*, said: 'there is not one such fossil for which one could make a watertight argument.'

And, Prof. Stephen J. Gould (1941-2002) said, 'The extreme rarity of transitional forms in the fossil record persists as the trade secret of paleontology.'

Indeed 150 years of vigorous searching by evolutionists through millions of tonnes (sic) of fossils has failed to produce even one clean 'chain' of such transitional forms, let alone the multitudes of chains required by Darwinism. Over the years only a tiny handful of 'candidates' claimed to be 'transitional' have been produced. These have usually been announced in a blaze of publicity to showcase evolution and indoctrinate everybody. However, when, with time, the weight of contrary evidence has indicated error, recantation (if any) has usually been whisper quiet, and the next generation of scientists promotes its own contenders." Russel Grigg, "Abandoned Transitional Forms" *Creation* Vol 33 No. 2 (2011): 12.

When the fossil record is objectively examined, there has never been an intermediate stage fossil that could withstand continued scrutiny and serve as proof of the "missing link" in the advancement from a lower state to a higher state in any organism. As a matter of fact, the fossil record shows multiple evidences that complex life was at the beginning of the fossil record, found right alongside simple life forms. Of course, this doesn't fit the evolutional theory and must be ignored.

Why? Because of the initial presumption of the archaeologist; that evolution is factual. Obvious contrary facts, although unexplainable in terms of their theory, and because they do not support their theory, are ignored. With rare exception, any find, or any lack of a finding, that fails to support their atheistic views, will simply be ignored.

But, it should be stated that just because evolution is a theory, that is not sufficient grounds on its own to completely discount it. There are other theories, such as Atomic Theory, Electron Theory, etc., that, when put to the test, just like gravity, prove to perform as theorized and to obey the mathematical principles applied to the theory.

Such is not the case with evolution. There are no reliable, repeatable, evidences. There are no fossil, mathematical, or observable occurrences, which support the theory of evolution as fact.

As previously stated, it requires such faith in the veracity of the theory, that observable facts to the contrary must be ignored. The widely accepted view of a vast complex system of fossils, ever increasing from a low state to a higher state, exists only in the imagination of the evolutionists and the artists who drew the charts.

"Dr. Colin Patterson (Senior Paleontologist of

the British Natural History Museum) has been quoted in many periodicals as asking the participants at a meeting of other international evolutionists: 'Can anyone tell me one indisputable fact about the theory of evolution?' When no hands were raised and no voices heard, Dr. Patterson continued, 'I can tell you one. It certainly should not be taught in public schools as a scientific fact.'"
Gary Bates, "That Quote!" *Creation;* Vol 29 No. 1 (2006): 13.

History is replete with examples of those who endorsed the secular humanist philosophy; which was principally generated by the theory of evolution.

Some of those "philosophers" were: Karl Marx, Adolf Hitler, Joseph Stalin, Pol Pot, etc.

The following details one of the founders of the legal process of sacrificing babies on the altar of convenience and selling baby parts as though they were autos in a salvage yard.

"Margaret Louise Sanger (1879 – 1966) was a birth control, population control, and eugenics activist. She changed the world, but for the worse.

By 1911, Sanger had moved to New York City, where she became heavily influenced by anarchist, socialist, and labor activists. She began *joining and participating* in radical groups and causes.

In March 1914, Sanger published the first issue of her own paper, *The Woman Rebel*. Along with providing information about birth control, Sanger wholeheartedly supported the use of violence to achieve political, economic, and social goals--case in point, the *Lexington Avenue bombing*. On July 4th of that year, a bomb accidentally exploded in a

Harlem apartment, killing three men and one woman. The three men were planning to bomb the home of industrialist John D. Rockefeller, but the bomb exploded prematurely. The plan was devised at the Ferrer Center, an educational institution, which also served as the meeting place for a movement of radicals. Sanger lectured at the institution, and was active in the movement.

After the failed terrorist attempt, Sanger wrote a *commentary,* calling the deaths a display of 'courage, determination, conviction, a spirit of defiance.' She argued the 'real tragedy' was 'the cowardice and the poisonous respectability' of the movement's leaders who offered apologies, rather than defiance, for the episode. Sanger urged those in the movement to 'accept and exult in every act of revolt against oppression,' including terrorist acts. She also published a *complementary article* that defended the assassination of political or industrial leaders.

The following month, August 1914, Sanger was *indicted* for inciting murder and assassination, and for violating obscenity laws. But instead of facing the charges, she fled the country. On the trip to England, after the ship had entered international waters, Sanger instructed her supporters to distribute 100,000 copies of her pamphlet, *Family Limitation*. In February 1916, the charges were dropped.

In October 1916, Sanger *opened* America's first birth control clinic. Located in Brownsville, New York, the clinic permanently closed a month later, after Sanger was charged with maintaining a public nuisance. In February 1917, she was convicted and given a thirty day prison sentence.

Also in February 1917, the first issue of Sanger's journal, *The Birth Control Review*, was published. She was *The Review*'s editor until 1929, and used her editorials to promote birth control and eugenics. For Sanger, these issues were inseparable.

The word *eugenics*, which means *well born*, was coined in 1883 by Sir Francis Galton, a cousin of Charles Darwin. Positive eugenics was a movement that attempted to "improve" the human population by encouraging "fit" people to reproduce. Negative eugenics, conversely, attempted to "improve" the human population by discouraging "unfit" people from reproducing. The "unfit" people included the poor, the sick, the disabled, the "feeble-minded," the "idiots," the "morons," and the "insane." And "discouragement" from reproducing included the use of force.

Sanger rejected positive eugenics, while embracing negative eugenics. She wrote, 'Like the advocates of Birth Control, the eugenists, for instance, are seeking to assist the race toward the elimination of the unfit. Both are seeking a single end but they lay emphasis upon different methods.' She stressed the need to merge eugenics with birth control, adding, 'Eugenics without Birth Control seems to us a house builded upon the sands. It is at the mercy of the rising stream of the unfit.'

And Sanger advocated birth control backed up by forced sterilization or segregation to achieve her aims, *writing*, 'While I personally believe in the sterilization of the feeble-minded, the insane and syphilitic, I have not been able to discover that these measures are more than superficial deterrents when applied to the constantly growing stream of the unfit. They are excellent means of meeting a certain phase of the situation, but I believe in regard to these, as in regard to other eugenic means, that they do not go to the bottom of the matter.' The bottom of the matter was *'to create a race of thoroughbreds'*. So the government, Sanger concluded, needed 'to apply a stern and rigid policy of sterilization and segregation to that grade of population whose progeny is already tainted, or whose inheritance is such that objectionable traits may be transmitted to offspring' and 'to give certain dysgenic groups in our population their choice of segregation or sterilization.'

In her 1920 book, *Woman and the New Race*, Sanger wrote that birth control 'is nothing more or less than the facilitation of the process of weeding out the unfit, of preventing the birth of defectives or of those who will become defectives.'

She had a plan. And she was about to get an organization. In 1921, Sanger *founded* the American Birth Control League, which (following a 1939 merger with the Birth Control Clinical Research Bureau and then a 1942 name change) became the Planned Parenthood Federation of America. While the organization was growing, the close association between the birth control movement and the eugenics movement had made a name change necessary. Nazi Germany had implemented *racial hygiene* policies, including mass sterilizations, inspired by the eugenics movement in America. So "birth control" was removed from the name to create a new public image. The agenda, though, stayed the same. And in 1948, Sanger helped *form* the International Committee on Planned Parenthood, which (in 1952) became the International Planned Parenthood Federation." (www.liveaction.org/research/**margaret-sanger-quotes**-history-and-biography)

If there was no creator, and if mankind is not the marvelous work of God, then there are no moral absolutes: No God—No sin.

If mankind is just the result of accident and mutation, what does it matter if society rids itself of undesirable accidents or mutations? Kill the insane, the ethnically different, the crippled, the malformed, the bed-ridden, the aged, unwanted babies, etc. If there was no creator, then there is no promise of an afterlife, no Heaven to gain, no Hell to shun.

If there was no Adam and Eve, then there is no original sin and we waste our time serving God. Jesus was called the second Adam. If there was no first Adam, Jesus was not the second. Jesus said, *"Haven't you read...that at the beginning the Creator 'made them male and female,'"* (Matt: 19:4). If evolution were true, it would make Jesus deceived at best, a liar at worst.

If we face not our creator at judgment, what difference does it make what we do in this life? What difference does it make if you take someone's life, or someone takes your life? Dr. Carl Weiland relates the following:

"The young male students, who embarked on a

killing spree at Columbine High School, certainly placed no value on life—not their's or others. The writing of one of them, found after the shooting, said words to the effect, 'Me and "V" (his accomplice) in September are going to kick natural selection up a few notches," meaning of course survival of the fittest. They had weapons, the other students did not." Dr. Carl Weiland, *Origins in the Modern World Why It Matters; a generation destroyed!* Lecture on DVD; Creation Ministries Intl. (2003).

The suicide rate among teens and young adults is soaring. Why? Without God, to them, life is nothing but a series of disappointments and a continuum of desperation.

There is a story told of a young freshman girl standing in the school's hallway looking confused. She was noticed by a friend who asked her if anything was wrong. The young girl replied, "I just found out in my biology class that I'm nothing special. I'm just the accidental results of some pond scum or something that evolved into human beings." Her friend sympathetically replied, "I know. I felt the same way. What's your next class?" The freshman girl replied, "Self-Esteem."

Secular humanism makes man to be his own god. He makes his own rules and takes the glory for any improvement in his circumstances.

Evolutionists claim that just the right conditions existed at a precise moment in the primordial ooze and a protein was developed that formed itself into a living cell. In the succeeding chapters we shall examine evidence that sheds significant light upon this specious claim.

The complexity of such an occurrence cannot

be overemphasized. In Darwin's era, a single cell was considered by many to be the beginning point, the fundamental formation for the construction of all life. His proposition was that an accidental combination of chemicals created the first living cell.

However, in recent years, with the aid of modern magnification capability, scientists have discovered a complexity within a single cell that has bewildered the entire scientific community.

Chapter Two

IRREDUCIBLE COMPLEXITY

Proverbs 139:14
*"I praise you because I am fearfully and
wonderfully made;
your works are wonderful, I know that full well."*

As discussed previously, irreducible complexity is one of the primary issues that the flawed theory of evolution cannot effectively deal with. We begin with a portion from Dr. Jonathon Sarfati:

"Molecular biologist Michael Denton, writing as a non-creationist skeptic of Darwinian evolution, explains some of the cell's complexity that modern biology has discovered. This shows that Darwin and Haeckel were naïve in the extreme:

'Perhaps in no other area of modern biology is the challenge, posed by the extreme complexity and ingenuity of biological adaptations, more apparent than in the fascinating new molecular world of the cell...To grasp the reality of life as it has been revealed by molecular biology, we must (meaning we would have to) magnify a cell a thousand million times until it is twenty kilometers in diameter and resembles a giant airship large enough to cover a great city like London or New York. What we would then see would be an object of unparalleled complexity and adaptive design. On the surface of the cell we would see millions of openings, like the port holes of a vast space ship, opening and closing to allow a continual stream of materials to flow in and out. If we were to enter one of the openings we would find ourselves in a world of supreme technology and bewildering complexity.

Is it really credible that random processes could have constructed a reality, the smallest element of which—a functional protein or gene—is complex beyond our own creative capacities? A reality which is the very antithesis of chance (in) which the level of ingenuity and complexity exhibited by the molecular machinery of life, even our most advanced artifacts appear clumsy. It would be an illusion to think that what we are aware of at present is any more than a fraction of the full extent of biological design. In practically every field of fundamental biological research, ever increasing levels of design and complexity are being revealed at an ever-accelerating rate.'" Sarfati, Dr. Jonathon; *By Design,* (Australia: Creation Book Publishers, 2006), 153-59.

Proteins: The Machines of Life

Proteins must be folded. It is the variety of shapes that determines what the protein's function will be.

But, predicting the right shape from a given sequence is one of the hardest problems for a supercomputer to solve. IBM built the world's most powerful supercomputer (dubbed *Blue Gene,* completed in 2005) to tackle the protein folding problems--the IBM website explains why:

'The scientific community considers protein folding one of the most significant 'grand

challenges'—a fundamental problem in science…
whose solution can be advanced only by applying
high-performance computing technologies.

Proteins control almost all cellular processes in
the human body. Comprising strings of amino acids
that are joined like links of a chain, a protein folds
into a highly complex, three-dimensional shape that
determines its function. Any change in shape
dramatically alters the function of a protein, and
even the slightest change in the folding process can
turn a desirable protein into a disease.'

However, despite the enormous computing
power, they estimated that it would still take about a
year for *Blue Gene* to finish its calculations and
model the folding of a simple protein. But the cell
takes less than a second!

(Further) The origin of life from non-life defies
probability. It would require:

1. 20 amino acids
2. 387 proteins (all folded properly for their
   function) for the simplest possible life
3. 10 conserved amino acids on average

Therefore, the chance is 10^{-3870} X log 20 = 10^{-5035}

[Ibid] 153-59. (comments in parenthesis are mine)

In layman's terms this means 1 chance in 1
with 5,035 zeroes behind it.

"As the heavens are higher than the earth, so
are my ways higher than your ways and my
thoughts than your thoughts" (Isaiah 55:9).

When we view the irreducible complexity of
such a miniscule element of life, and we are faced
with the intricacies of design that cause the

organism to function on its own, are we surprised when the factors cry out, "Design demands a designer!?" If many thousands of years from now, and the earth continues to exist, and archaeologists dig down into the earth and find two items: For instance: A horse drawn cart and a 400 horsepower Mustang, will they then conclude that the horse, over thousands of years mutated into a V8? Did the cart mutate into the plush air conditioned body of the car?

Both have a source of power, both have wheels and axles, both carried people. But because the archaeologists shall have witnessed other "evolutionary" advances, all based upon the reasoning effort and intellect of humans, who over time, engineered and improved many manners of conveyance, they will conclude that a designer was involved. Yet neither vehicle can approach the complexity in design and function of a single human cell.

Problems arise for the Church when articles and books containing information to refute the atheistic view sit on the shelf unread. Again, Christians are likely to say, "Oh, I don't know about all of that. I just believe the Bible." Well, that is fine for the individual believer, if they choose to ignore the weapons provided by other Christians, but what about for the sake of our children and young college age adults?

Christianity has never been all about the individual. Jesus commissioned us all to go and teach. We don't send soldiers, sailors, and airmen, into battle unprepared. As the situations change the

battle plans must change. So it is with the Church. What was totally effective in 1950 simply doesn't meet the challenges of today's world.

The examples of irreducible complexity in nature are so many one could probably fill the remaining pages of this book with examples and explanations; the human eye, a bird's wing, or the ATP synthase enzyme motor, etc. We are not at the mercy of science; unless we remain ignorant of our own information.

Robert Jastrow was a famous scientist who is often quoted as follows:

"For the scientist who has lived by his faith in the power of reason, the story ends like a bad dream. He has scaled the mountain of ignorance. He is about to conquer the highest peak. As he pulls himself over the final rock, he is greeted by a band of theologians who have been sitting there for centuries." Robert Jastrow, *God and the Astronomer*, (New York: W.W. Norton 1978)

The Apostle Paul wrote:

"...what may be known about God is plain to them, because God has made it plain to them. For since the creation of the world God's invisible qualities—His eternal power and divine nature—have been clearly seen, being understood from what has been made, so that men are without excuse" (Romans 1:19-20).

Jerry Bergman writes:

"Richard Errett Smalley (1942-2005), MA, PhD, from Princeton, a professor of chemistry, physics, and astronomy at Rice University was awarded the Nobel Prize in chemistry in 1996 for his discovery of a new form of carbon comprised of soccer-ball shaped molecules.

Many researchers date the dawn of the modern nanotechnology field to Dr. Smalley's discovery. He received eight honorary Doctor of Science degrees.

As a scientist, Dr. Smalley searched for answers that made sense. At first, he could not accept the idea that the Bible was true and did not think science was compatible with Christianity. He attended a lecture presented at Rice on Intelligent Design. This lecture prompted him to look into evolution in detail. His reaction to what he was learning was anger. His wife (a biologist who had to come to terms with the same issues) stated that her husband hated bad science and that he would pace the bedroom floor in anger saying that evolution was bad science, claiming that if he had jumped to conclusions, as did the evolutionists, in his world he would have no respect within his scientific community.

After studying the issue in great detail, Dr. Smalley became an outspoken anti-Darwinist. In 2004 he delivered an anti-Darwinist address at Tuskegee University and received a standing ovation when he finished. In the lecture, he said: "The burden of proof is on those who don't believe that 'Genesis' was right and there was a creation, and that the Creator is still involved…"

He also claimed that Darwinian evolution had been given its death blow due to the advance of genetics and cell-biology, and that it was now clear that **biological evolution could not have occurred"** (emphasis added).

Jerry Bergman, "From Skepticism to Faith in Christ: a Nobel laureate's Journey; *Creation* Vol 33, No.2, (2011): 42-3

Douglas F. Kelly contends:

"The incredibly complex structures of living systems not only rule out gradual evolution by mutation and natural selection, they also require absolute creation; that is, being made 'full grown' or fully functional...the ordering of separate, well fitted components to achieve a function that is beyond any of the components themselves... (makes it) ...clear that if something was not put together gradually, then it must have been put together quickly or even suddenly.

There is only one way for massive intellectual, moral and cultural healing to occur, and it entails a revolutionary 'paradigm shift' from mythological evolution to a Scripturally revealed and scientifically realistic paradigm of special divine creation...and a growing chorus of voices from operational science confirms it."

Douglas F. Kelly, *Creation and Change* (Scotland: Christian Focus Publications 2010), 57.

No discussion of irreducible complexity would be complete without the examination of one of God's most marvelous little creatures; the Bombardier Beetle. The following is an excerpt from the on-line Encyclopedia *Wikipedia:*

"The bombardier beetle produces and stores two reactant chemical compounds;

hydroquinone and hydrogen peroxide. He keeps them in two separate reservoirs within his body. When threatened, the beetle contracts muscles in his abdomen that forces the two chemicals, from the reservoirs, through tubes, into a mixing chamber within the after part of his body. This chamber contains water and a mixture of catalytic enzymes. When combined, the reactants undergo a violent exothermic chemical reaction that raises the temperature of the chemicals in the mixing chamber to nearly the boiling point of water. The corresponding pressure build-up forces the entrance valves, from the reactant chemical storage chambers, to close. This protects the beetle's inner organs.

The boiling and foul-smelling liquid partially becomes a gas and is expelled through an outlet valve, or exhaust pipe, in the beetle's posterior. When propelled into the atmosphere it explodes with a loud popping sound.

The force of the explosion, if occurring all at once, would be destructive to the beetle. Therefore, the flow of reactants into the reaction or mixing chamber, and subsequent ejection into the atmosphere, occurs cyclically at a rate of approximately 1000 times per second, but the entire pulsation period lasts for only a fraction of a second. The explosive sound outside the beetle's body, combined with the smell, usually discourages predators from disturbing the beetle." Wikipedia, the Free Encyclopedia; Article: Bombardier beetle; www.wikipedia.org; accessed Dec. 20, 2011

Of course, the evolutionist would claim,

"millions of years, mutations and adaptations, and survival of the fittest." But, is that a sufficient answer to the following questions?

- Where did the beetle get storage tanks?
- Where did the beetle get the mixing chamber?
- Where did the beetle get the chemicals?
- How did he know which chemicals to get?
- Where did he get the catalytic enzymes?
- How did he know which ones to get?
- How many times did he blow the posterior off his body before he got the timing sequence figured out?
- Where did he go to school to study chemistry?

The constant claim of millions or billions of years must be addressed as well. Dr. Greenberg gives his opinion of the length of time required to make sandy beaches.

"For the past six years, Greenberg has focused his microscopes on common objects, such as grains of sand, flowers, and food. These everyday objects take on a new reality when magnified hundreds of times. His images of sand make us realize that **as we walk along a beach we are strolling on millions of years of biological and geological history**. He believes that art is a window through which we can appreciate the miracles of nature.

Dr. Greenberg is the featured artist at the Science Museum of Minnesota. His exhibit, "Exploring the Microscopic World of Sand Grains" will run from May 2008 through January 2010. He has recently written a fascinating book about sand grains through the microscope: *A Grain of Sand: Nature's Secret Wonder,* Voyageur Press, Minneapolis, 2008." Wikipedia the Free Encyclopedia; Article: *Sand Beaches*; (Jan 26, 2012).

Enter the Island of Surtsey; born in 1963:

"Surtsey (Icelandic, meaning "Surtur's island") is a volcanic island off the southern coast of Iceland. At Coordinates: 63°18'11"N 20°36'17"W 63.303°N 20.6047°W it is also the southernmost point of Iceland. It was formed in a volcanic eruption which began 130 meters (426 ft) below sea level, and reached the surface on 15 November 1963. The eruption lasted until 5 June 1967, when the island reached its maximum size of 2.7 km^2 (1.0 sq mi).

Since the end of the eruption, erosion has seen the island diminish in size. A large area on the south-east side has been eroded away completely, **while a sand spit called *Norðurtangi* (north point) has grown on the north side of the island.** It is estimated that about 0.024 km^3 (0.0058 cu mi) of material has been lost due to erosion – this represents about a quarter of the original above-sea-level volume of the island."

Wikipedia The Free Encyclopedia; Article: Surtsey Island (Accessed Feb 2, 2012).

Not millions, or perhaps billions, of years: A sandy beach within 20 years. The Church can fight back if they become armed with facts.

However, Satan doesn't have to disprove the existence of God to win; he just has to instill sufficient doubt. As Peter found while walking on the water with Jesus, doubt destroys faith. Like Peter, Christianity will become imperiled by the waves of opposition if the Church begins to embrace a secular view of the wondrous works of God.

Darwin stated in his book *Origin of Species*, that should it ever be proven that there are no evolutionary life form fossils found beneath the earth's Cambrian strata, where complex life forms of all varieties just suddenly appear in the true fossil record, often referred to as the "Cambrian Explosion," then his theory would be totally without substance.

Well, guess what, they have examined the layer below the Cambrian, no evolutionary life forms!! Has this information penetrated the dogged defense of those such as the celebrated atheistic evolutionist Richard Dawkins? No, it is simply ignored. His only recourse is the dogma of Socialism: Accuse Christians of being stupid, dogmatic, ignorant of science, lacking facts, etc. But does he ever offer proof to support his disputations? The Church must stand up and be counted, armed with truth and without fear, proclaiming to the world that there can be no compromise—no theistic evolution and no millions or billions of years of chance and change.

The Church cannot have one foot in the Holy Word and one foot in the Humanist philosophy of the world, except to understand the humanist philosophy and know enough science to refute it.

The more the Church tries to accommodate the world the more the world will despise us. Jesus has a message for those who accommodate the world: "I know your deeds, that you are neither cold nor hot. I wish you were either one or the other! So, because you are lukewarm—neither hot nor cold—I am about to spit you out of my mouth" (Rev 3:15).

That Scripture needs some illumination. The city of Laodicea obtained its water supply from some warm springs in the hills above the city. It was piped down to the city through clay pipes and of course upon arrival was a tepid temperature not readily accepted by the palate. Therefore, Jesus is not saying he wishes that they were hot Christians or cold Christians literally. He is saying that the Laodicean Christians were like their water, which in order to be palatable needed to be hot or cold. It was a metaphor that the Laodiceans understood very well. He was basically saying that they may be talking the talk, but, He wanted them to walk the walk.

That would be sage advice today for many churches that have the reputation of being representatives of Christ, but have no substantive works to show for it.

Churches are now ordaining practicing homosexuals and endorsing life styles that ought to be brought to the altar, confessed, and cleansed.

Chapter Three

SECULAR HUMANISM INFILTRATES THE SCHOOLS AND THE COURTS

II Timothy 4: 3-4
"For the time will come when men will not put up with sound doctrine. Instead, to suit their own desires, they will gather around them a great number of teachers to say what their itching ears want to hear. They will turn their ears away from the truth and turn aside to myth."

In this chapter we shall examine the history of court decisions in our country that have gradually and consistently eroded our influence on public education. It is an ongoing program. Knowing about it is a start, but it will not stem the tide against us unless we stand for what we believe and vote for the principles of our faith--and not the well-being of our finances.

The First Constitutional Amendment, often erroneously described as Separation of Church and State, was put in place to protect the various religions from infringement and dictatorial mandates by the State. Christians not only have every right to engage in politics, they have an obligation to do so. That's where a major battle field lies. We have to engage the atheistic legal system and special interest groups in order to defeat them.

Clucking our tongues and wondering, "What ever happened to this country?" is how we got into the predicament we're in. Christians need to attend school board meetings, serve on boards, support candidates who support Christian principles, and stress involvement to other Christians—with prudent regard for the confines of the law.

The moral majority is rapidly disappearing in this country. The silent majority can no longer remain silent, unless we wish to forfeit the very reasons for which the pilgrims came to America—religious freedom.

The issues cited herein need to be addressed from the pulpits, in the Sunday school classes, and in Bible studies. In this writer's opinion, if Christians who give are more worried about a tax deductible gift to the Church, under 501c3, than they are about ensuring they are a moral voice in politics and the truth of the Word is upheld, regardless of who does, or does not, like it, then perhaps they are giving for the wrong reasons.

Jesus said to his disciples, not long after His teaching on the Beatitudes, "and from the days of John the Baptist until now, the kingdom of the heaven is forcibly treated and the forceful men seize it" (John 11:12 The Nestle Greek Text)

Never, since the pilgrims landed in America, has Christianity, in the United States, had to contend for its faith as it has needed to do in recent times. "One nation under God" has come into question from many sources. Minority voices have been busy, like so many termites, undermining the foundation upon which our nation was built. It is time for us to awake, arouse ourselves, flood on to the battle field, and hold our ground—before we are forcefully silenced.

Atheists Begin the Struggle

Norman Geisler writes an excellent synopsis of the beginnings of what he terms the "evolution revolution:"

"Charles Darwin started the evolution revolution. There were evolutionists before Darwin, even in ancient times, but Darwin was the first to propose a plausible scientific mechanism by which evolution could have occurred. Between the 1859 publication of his landmark volume *On the Origin of Species* and 1900, the naturalistic macroevolution theory literally conquered the intellectual scientific world of the West.

From the beginning, serious religious and moral implications were apparent in Darwin's theory. Darwin himself called it 'my deity... Natural Selection.' The very subtitle of his book, referring to the "preservation of favoured races in the struggle for life," has racial implications.

Darwin's friend Karl Marx declared, 'But nowadays, in our evolutionary conception of the universe, there is absolutely no room for either a creator or a ruler.'" Norman Geisler, *Creation and the Courts;* (Wheaton, IL: Crossway Books, 2007), 31-2.

In America there were a few strong voices who spoke out against this theory calling it atheistic. No design, no designer, no creation, no creator, no higher power, no God, these were all features of

Darwinism that were criticized by some scientists of the day. Darwinism was not really taken seriously by the religious community in general until some 60 years later--after the rise of Adolf Hitler:

"Perhaps the most frightening consequences of Darwinism were the ethical ones. In 1924 a young Adolf Hitler wrote *Mein Kampf,* in which he proposed, following the example of evolution...weeding out the weaker breeds of mankind. And he proceeded to put his proposal into action, exterminating those he considered less fit. Hitler justified his action by evolution, claiming, 'If Nature does not wish that weaker individuals should mate with the stronger, she wishes even less that a superior race should intermingle with an inferior one; because in such a case all her efforts, throughout hundreds of thousands of years, to establish an evolutionary higher stage of being, may thus be rendered futile.'

One year after Hitler's racist book, the people of Tennessee passed the Butler Act on March 13, 1925, forbidding the teaching of evolution in the public schools. Interestingly, the biology textbook that had been used in the schools before this, taught racism similar to Hitler's views." Ibid., p. 33.

A quote from *Mein Kampf*:

"At the present time there exists upon the earth five races...These are the Ethiopian or negro type, originating in Africa; the Malay or brown race, from the islands of the Pacific; the American Indian; the Mongolian or yellow race, including the natives of China, Japan, and the Eskimos; and finally the highest type of all, the Caucasians, represented by the civilized white inhabitants of Europe and America." Ibid, p.33

Egomania in its most repulsive form.

The passing of the Butler Act of March 1925 provided an opportunity for the ACLU to generate one of the most famous trials in the history of the United States; the Scopes trial of July 1925. The ACLU was eager for an opportunity to challenge this new law in Tennessee. They advertised throughout the state for someone who would be willing to break the law. John Scopes, a young teacher, volunteered to do so.

William Jennings Bryan faced off against Clarence Darrow. Perhaps one of the most telling statements made at that trial, as far as the Church is concerned was made by Bryan: "If all biologists in the world teach this doctrine, as Mr. Darrow says they do, then may heaven defend the youth of our land from their impious babblings." Ibid., p.34

The trial lasted for eight days and the decision rendered in Dayton, Tennessee was that it was illegal to teach evolution in the public schools of that state.

Hollywood made a movie, and a travesty, of the trial called: *Inherit the Wind.* Spencer Tracy was the star who played the part of the agnostic Clarence Darrow. The movie of course portrayed him as the slick and crafty city lawyer versus the fundamentalist, narrow-minded, unscientific, semi-buffoon, William Jennings Bryan. Of course, the actual transcripts describe no such atmosphere.

But what the Scopes trial did was open the door for lawsuits in other cases and other states.

Tennessee was not the only state that had anti-evolution laws. Similar laws were passed in Oklahoma, Florida, and Texas. Between 1921 and 1929 such bills were introduced in twenty states. Some of the notable cases that followed were:

(1) The Epperson Ruling in 1968 in Arkansas wherein the Supreme Court ruled that it was a violation of the First amendment to forbid the teaching of evolution in public schools.

(2) The Segraves Ruling in 1981 a superior court in California ruled that discussing evolution in public school did not violate the children's right to freedom of religion.

(3) The McLean Ruling of 1982 mandated that it was not necessary to teach creation alongside evolution in Arkansas.

(4) Mozert v. Hawkins County Board of Education in 1987 – Students and parents claimed a violation of First Amendment rights to free exercise of religion when forced by the school board to read school books which teach or inculcate values in violation of their religious beliefs and convictions. Sixth Circuit Court ruled there was no evidence that anyone was ever required to affirm or believe any idea or practice taught in the text or the class.

(5) The Edwards Ruling in 1987 in Louisiana concerned an Act passed, that provided for teaching evolution and creation in a balanced way in public schools. This resulted in the highest court ruling: "The Act impermissibly endorses religion by advancing the religious belief that a supernatural being created humankind."

(6 +) The Webster Ruling in 1990; The Peloza

v Capistrano Ruling 1994; The Freiler Ruling 1997; The LeVake Ruling 2000; and The Dover Ruling 2005; which was the first test for the teaching of Intelligent Design.

The ruling was: Intelligent Design and Creation are not science and should not be taught in Dover, PA classes. Intelligent design and other forms of creation are essentially religious and are, therefore, a violation of the First Amendment. Ibid., p. 79-238

It is obvious that the precedents have been long established. The public schools are not likely to accommodate the Church's views, or the views of individual Christians. Therefore, it is a vital issue for the Church to ensure that our children are armed with information about creation as well as faith in God's Word.

Faith in God is predicated upon three general principles:

(1) Knowledge: We must know and learn about God.

(2) Belief: We must believe the knowledge we have received about God is true.

(3) Trust: We must be willing to act upon what we know, believing that God is totally trustworthy.

As an example: If one is on foot traveling through a great forest and comes upon an un-crossable great ravine and sees that a tree has fallen across it, one may wish to cross upon that tree. That satisfies the first step of faith. One knows the tree is across the ravine. The second step would be to examine the tree and determine if one believes that the tree is strong enough to hold the weight of the one to cross upon it. When one believes that the tree is strong enough, the second step is complete. Now, the third step is to get up on the tree and walk to the other side, "trusting" and walking "in faith" upon what one knows about the tree and believes about the tree. But, until one is walking on that tree, just having the knowledge and the belief isn't going to get one to the other side.

Faith in evolution is not different: knowledge, belief, and action.

However, one system of faith is based upon truth and one is not. Evolutionists are walking in belief and faith without any real knowledge and truth to back it up. Knowledge of truth is the key-- not mere supposition. Faith ungrounded in knowledge is headed for a fall.

Today, in the Church, a view arises known as "Theistic Evolution" as previously mentioned. Even one of the most outspoken critics of Christianity, Richard Dawkins, an ardent supporter of evolution, recognizes that there can be no compromise between creation and evolution. When he was asked why and when he made up his mind that God doesn't exist, he answered:

"Oh, well, by far the most important, I suppose, was understanding evolution. I think the evangelical Christians have really sort of got it right, in a way, in seeing evolution as the enemy. Whereas the more—what shall we say—sophisticated theologians who are quite happy to live with evolution, I think they're deluded. I think the evangelicals have got it right, in that there really is a deep incompatibility between evolution and

Dr. Jerry Terrebrood

Christianity, and I think I realized that at the age of about sixteen." Lita Cosner and Gary Bates, "A Hostile Witness;" *Creation Ministries International Prayer News* UPDATE; (Powder Springs, GA: Nov 2011):

Dawkins then ridiculed the interviewer, Howard Condor from *Revelation TV* in the United Kingdom, by asking:

"Why on earth would ... you believe in Genesis, given that the Archbishop of Canterbury is against it, given that the Pope is against it, any respectable bishop is against it?" Ibid.

In the Book of Acts the Apostle Paul is preaching in Athens to some who were Epicurean and Stoic philosophers interested in the "foreign god" about which Paul was speaking. They took Paul to a meeting of the Areopagus, where they questioned him concerning this new teaching. The Bible states that all the Athenians and the foreigners who lived there spent their time doing nothing but talking about and listening to the latest ideas. These could certainly be described as seekers of knowledge.

Knowledge in and of itself is not always truth. Knowledge, whether gained by study or experience, helps one to judge that which is true from that which is false. Facts are considered to be true. Yet, not everything considered to be true is a fact. Truth sometimes suffers at the hands of the majority. Truth is not a democratic experience. The majority may believe, and historically have believed, many things to be true, which are actually false. Many facts have lain undetected, undetermined, not understood, or not believed, for exceptionally long periods of time. What shall we deduce from the foregoing?

The Athenians, who were notorious seekers after knowledge, had erected a monument "To the Unknown God." Some have ventured that they did so to make sure they didn't errantly leave out any of the gods whether they had thought of them or not. Or, perhaps they recognized that despite all of their seeking, and all of their knowledge, there was still a power far greater than them, by which all things have their being.

Paul says to them: "The God who made the world and everything in it is the Lord of heaven and earth and does not live in temples built by hands. And he is not served by human hands, as if he needed anything, because he himself gives all men life and breath and everything else. From one man he made every nation of men that they should inhabit the whole earth; and he determined the times set for them and the exact places where they should live. God did this so that men would seek him and perhaps reach out for him and find him, being, as some of your own poets have said, 'We are his children'" (Acts 17:24-28).

The Bible doesn't leave a Christian any choices. If Genesis is false, Jesus was false, Paul was false, and all other references to the book of Genesis in the Bible are false—whether the Pope agrees, the Archbishop of Canterbury, or any "respectable" bishop agrees.

A major problem with knowledge is that many who possess it are somewhat cerebrally inflated concerning it and consider the knowledge that they have to be absolute--bordering on infallible. Few entertain the possibility that they may be deceived by cleverly contrived theories or un-provable assumptions.

Someone may ask me; isn't it possible that you are deceived? To which I would respond: Were it not for the many infallible proofs I have in my experience with faith in the immutable Word of God and my personal relationship with the Father, the Son, and the Holy Spirit, I would admit to the possibility. But, no man made contrivance, theory, delusion, or illusion, could produce what I have witnessed in my Christian life regarding changed lives, prayers answered, and miraculous events. One may wish to peruse my book *But Wait! There's More!* at online retailers such as amazon.com, barnesandnoble.com and alibris.com. And yet, I freely admit, I have not scratched the surface of knowledge where the works of God are concerned.

The Church must stand its ground in defense and support of the Word. Again the Apostle Paul writes, this time in I Corinthians 1:18-29:

"For the message of the cross is foolishness to those who are perishing, but to us who are being saved it is the power of God. For it is written: 'I will destroy the wisdom of the wise; the intelligence of the intelligent I will frustrate.' Where is the wise man? Where is the scholar? Where is the philosopher of this age? Has not God made foolish the wisdom of the world? For since in the wisdom of God the world through its wisdom did not know him, God was pleased through the foolishness of what was preached to save those who believe…For the foolishness of God is wiser than man's wisdom, and the weakness of God is stronger than man's strength. Brothers, think of what you were when you were called. Not many of you were wise by human standards; not many were influential; not many were of noble birth. But God chose the foolish things of the world to shame the wise; God chose the weak things of the world to shame the strong. He chose the lowly things of this world and the despised things—and the things that are not—to nullify the things that are, so that no one may boast before him."

Paul continues in chapter 2 verses 12-14: "We have not received the spirit of the world but the Spirit who is from God, that we may understand what God has freely given us. This is what we speak, not in words taught us by human wisdom but in words taught by the Spirit, expressing spiritual truths in spiritual words. **The man without the Spirit does not accept the things that come from the Spirit God, for they are foolishness to him, and he <u>cannot</u> understand them, because they are spiritually discerned"** (bold letters added for emphasis).

In the passage quoted above, the portion "he cannot understand them," is literally rendered in the Greek, *"ou* (he) *dunatai* (cannot or impossible) *gnonai* (to know) *'oti* (because) *pneumatikos* (spiritually) *avakrinetai* (examined or investigated prior to judgement).

The rendering in the NIV as quoted above is not wrong. But, in my humble opinion, there is more stated here for us to consider. I think that a pivotal portion is the use of the words *gnonai* and *anakrinetai.* The word *gnonai* signifies knowing as a fact when coupled with *anakrinetai*. When taken together they mean to make a complete investigation of the facts prior to making a judgment. This word *avakrinetai* in particular is used only in Acts by Luke and in Corinthians by Paul.

Both portions of Corinthians quoted above are leading us to conclude: You don't need advanced secular education to understand the works of God. But, you will never truly know, even by close scrutiny, without doubt, until God reveals to you by His Spirit the wonders of His magnificent creation and His wondrous works among men.

Knowledge is similar to the possession of a large chest of tools. If a carpenter is in the proper element for working with wood and building structures made of wood and nails, he is well prepared for the job with his chest of tools. If however, the job is to disassemble and overhaul the workings of a foreign automobile, with all metric fittings, the carpenter finds he is unable to help because the tools in his chest are not the proper ones for the job at hand.

So it is with knowledge stemming from secular humanist thought. When thinking of a world that was invented for and by one's own presumptions, it all seems logical. Yet, upon close examination, the world is far more complex and far more intricately designed by processes that are far beyond man's finding out; a job for which the humanist does not have the tools. However, once having accepted the basic humanist premise that there is no God; man is left in a trap of his own making

PART II

THE FOUNDING FATHERS AND A
CHRISTIAN NATION

I Peter 2:15-17

*For it is God's will that, by doing good, you should silence the
ignorant talk of foolish men. Live as free men, but do not use
your freedom as a cover up for evil; live as servants of God.
Show proper respect to everyone: Love the brotherhood of
believers, fear God, honor the King.*

Nothing in the whole of this treatise should be
viewed as an appeal for Christian anarchy. Rather it
inveighs against the historical inaction of the
Christian community while there was yet time to
preclude many of the opinions, court decisions, and
legislative actions that have been levied against the
Church. Not only is the church not blameless on

those accounts, but history reveals that the Church was often its own worst enemy through insistence upon rigid and inflexible "religious" views; having more to do with a particular denominational bias than with the spiritual intent of the Bible.

Nor is there any intention to place the Bible in some secondary light where argument for creation and against evolution is required. Much of the world has lost confidence in the Bible. Bringing just the Bible to the forefront of the war may be premature.

Christians need to turn Satan's own tactics against him. Armed with sufficient scientific data, in support of creation, and against evolution, Christians can engender doubt in the minds of the secular humanist. Once that doubt takes root, the questions that follow will bring the Bible into play at the right moment and the right atmosphere.

We live in a democratic society, but, oftentimes the minority voice is heard far more often and more loudly than is the voice of what was once the Christian majority in this country. We are still a democracy.

My aim is to say: Christians need to unite and participate in this democracy instead of sitting at home wondering, "How did we let this happen?" I place myself in the mix as well. Although, I have voted in state and national elections, I haven't involved myself in politics at the school board, city, or county levels. But, I do support organizations such as ACLJ who can go and do far more than I could on my own.

The last few years have certainly amplified the

need for Christian unity. History will reveal however, there has always been a need. Many believe that "Separation of Church and State" is a statement in the constitution. IT IS NOT. IT NEVER HAS BEEN.

When I began studying American History in public school, not long after WWII, it was made clear to me that the pilgrims came to America to escape religious persecution in their own countries; mainly by the Church of England and Roman Catholicism. It was stated plainly in the history books that "America was founded upon the principles of religious freedom."

Many years later, as I studied for my bachelor's degree, the history books claimed that America was founded upon the principles of "glory and gold." My professor stated that he, without reservation, personally disagreed with that view. All of his studies revealed the first premise to be true but, we needed to be exposed to what the revisionists had done to our nation's history.

Currently, because of an unrealistic trend toward what has been called "political correctness," we graduate many high-school students who have difficulty comprehending what they read neither can they write intelligently or effectively, because we don't want to injure their self-esteem.

As the College Director of ITT Tech in Houston, TX, I had to offer a free six week remedial course in Mathematics, which began with basic Arithmetic, before many of the Texas High School graduates could begin the study of Electronic Engineering Technology. Similar results were encountered at Springfield College in Missouri, but the curricula being taught at Springfield College was not so technically demanding as is Electronics Engineering Technology.

Also, in the name of "political correctness," people who are unqualified in many areas are given preferential treatment for jobs and admission to college, with no one keeping an eye on the poor results of such a philosophy. How "politically correct" is it when they have failed in a collegiate system that they were unprepared for? How does that affect their self-esteem? What is the usual result? Is it a change in the preferential treatment policy, or, is it a cry for lower standards in the curriculum to accommodate their self-esteem?

With 22 years of military background, I know from experience: it is to your peril if you ever lower your standards to accommodate the level of those who must meet them—you must always elevate performers to the standard.

Using that premise as an example, we must work to hold our government to the standards of our forefathers and the U.S. Constitution as it was written and intended; based upon Godly principles and not as it is modified by minority humanist interpretation.

Here we are speaking of the contract entered into by the founding citizens of this country, to which every immigrant coming into this nation was sworn to uphold, before being offered citizenship.

Dee Wampler is an attorney who practices and resides in Springfield, Missouri. Although he has a stellar reputation in law, he is also a student of history and in the book cited below, rises to the defense of the Constitution and brings truth to the laws meant to protect our Christian heritage. The following are excerpts from his book:

"The *Arbella* landed in the spring of 1630 with the future leaders of the Massachusetts Bay Colony. John Winthrop preaching to fellow passengers stated: We shall be as a City upon a Hill, the eyes of all the people are upon us; so that if we shall deal falsely with our god in this work, we have undertaken and so cause him to withdraw his present help from us we shall be made a story and by-word through the world." Dee Wampler, *The Myth of Separation of Church And State*, (Enumclaw, WA: WinePress Publishing: 2004) 17

Wampler cites the statements of the first Governor of the Massachusetts Bay Colony William Bradford (1590-1657). He writes about the establishment of the colony in what has come to be called the Bradford Manuscript:

"I must begin at the very root and rise of the same. I shall endeavor to manifest in plain style the simple truth in all things…to have the right worship of God and discipline of Christ established in church, according to the simplicity of the Gospel without the mixture of men's inventions; and to have and be ruled by the laws of God's Word" Ibid., p. 18

Sir William Blackstone (1723-1780) was an English barrister whose eighteenth commentary of the law is perhaps one of the most famous law books ever written. When I was serving as the

Dr. Jerry Terrebrood

President of Springfield College in Springfield, Mo., our legal department had a complete set of Blackstone in the Library both in book form and computer application software. In writing of the nature of law he stated:

"This will of his maker is called the law of nature. God as God, when he created matter, and inured it with the principle of mobility, established certain rules. So when He created man, and inured (him) with free will to conduct himself in all parts of life, he laid down certain immutable laws of human nature. Considering the creator only a being of infinite power...and of infinite wisdom, he has laid down only such laws as were founded in those relations of justice, that existed in the nature of things antecedent to any positive precept. These are the eternal, immutable laws of good and evil to which the creator himself and all his dispensations conforms... the law of nature, being coequal with mankind and dictated by God himself, is of course superior in obligation to any other. It is binding over all the globe and all countries, and all times: no human laws are of any validity if contrary to this."
Ibid., p. 24-5.

George Washington, our first President, said these words in his inaugural address:

"It would be peculiarly improper to omit, in this first official act, my fervent supplication to that Almighty Being, who presides over the universe, who presides in the counsels of nations, and whose provincial aids can supply every human defect, that His benediction may consecrate to the liberties and happiness of the people of the United States...every step by which they have advanced to the character of an independent nation seems to have been distinguished by some token of providential agency...we ought to be no less persuaded that the propitious smiles of Heaven can never be expected on a nation that disregards the eternal rules of order and right, which heaven itself has ordained." Ibid., p. 28.

"John Adams insisted July 4th should be remembered as a 'Day of Deliverance by solemn acts of devotion to God Almighty.'

By 1776, ninety-eight percent of all Americans professed to be Protestant Christians. If this is not a Christian nation, how was it originally founded? The U.S. Supreme Court has made this pact clear throughout the centuries. In 1892 they held: 'These references add a volume of unofficial declarations to the massive organic utterances that this is a religious people...a Christian nation.'

One extremist said: 'providence has given to our people the choice of their ruler and it is the duty as well as the privilege and interest of our Christian nation to select and prefer Christians for our rulers.' Who was this extremist and shouldn't he apologize for his statements–as being politically incorrect? It was the Honorable John Jay, the first Chief Justice of the United States Supreme Court and author of the *Federalist Papers.*" Ibid., p. 29-30.

The following quotes, also from Wampler's book, are critically germane:

"*Benjamin Franklin to the Constitutional congress, June 28, 1787:* In the beginning of the contest with Great Britain, when we were sensible of danger, we had daily prayers in this room for divine protection. Our prayers were heard and they were graciously answered...Have we now forgotten this powerful friend? Or do we no longer need his assistance? I have lived a long time, Sir, and the longer I live, the more convincing proofs I see of this truth: That God governs the affairs of man. And, if a sparrow cannot fall to the ground without his notice, is it probable that an empire can rise without His aid?" Ibid p. 71

Thomas Jefferson: "In matters of religion, I have considered that its free exercise is placed by the Constitution independent of the powers of the General Government. I have therefore undertaken, on no occasion, to prescribe the religious exercise suited to it; but have left them as the Constitution found them, under the direction and discipline of the state and church authorities." Ibid p. 71

George Washington: "Whereas, it is the duty of all nations to acknowledge the providence of the Almighty God, to obey his will, to be grateful for His benefits, and humbly implore his protection and favor..." Ibid. p. 72.

John Quincy Adams: "The first and almost the only book deserving of universal attention is the Bible." Ibid.

Abraham Lincoln: "All the good from the Saviour of the world is communicated through this Book; but for the Book we could not know right from wrong. All the things desirable to man are contained in it." Ibid. p. 73

Woodrow Wilson: "The Bible is the one supreme source of revelation of the meaning of life, the nature of God and spiritual nature and needs of men. It is the only guide of life which really leads the spirit in the way of peace and salvation." Ibid. p. 73

Andrew Jackson.: "Go to the Scriptures…the joyful promise it contains will be a balsam to all your troubles." Ibid. p. 75.

Calvin Coolidge: "The foundations of our society and our government rest so much on the teachings of the Bible that it would be difficult to support them in faith if these teachings would cease to be practically universal in our country." Ibid. p. 75

President Theodore Roosevelt: "I believe the next half-century will determine if we will advance the cause of Christian civilization or revert to the horrors of brutal paganism." Ibid. p. 125.

There can be no doubt, when we examine history, that this was in the beginning, a Christian nation, it was intended to always be a Christian nation, and if Christians rise up without fear, and participate, as is their democratic right in this great republic, it shall ever be a Christian nation.

As discussed previously, too many religious organizations believe that the government, in the form of the IRS, or some other bureau, has the right to dictate what is preached in our churches.

Wampler continues:

"The U.S. Supreme court has continually held that, above all else, the First Amendment means that government has no power to restrict expression because of its message, ideas, subject matter, or content.

Attempts to stifle Christian voices generally fail the constitutional test. However, all too frequently, Christians back down at even the first hint of oppression. We cannot afford to retreat from

Dr. Jerry Terrebrood

the streets and the halls of government. We cannot afford to turn the marketplace of ideas over to those who are ignorant or even hostile to our faith.

We must stop taking our constitutional liberties for granted and take them back. Now, more than ever, we need to not only defend our rights, but to go on the offensive.

We are on the threshold of major change in our country. Our continued and stepped-up involvement is critical to channel the momentum towards true liberty and we must impact our culture for Christ." Ibid. p. 135.

The following statements from members of the Supreme Court are also essential to this discussion:

"The Constitution (does not) require complete separation of church and state; it forbids hostility toward any:" *Chief Justice Warren Burger in Lynch Vs. Donnelly*, 465 U.S. 668 (1984) Ibid. p.136.

"Devout Christians are destined to be regarded as fools in modern society. We are fools for Christ's sake. We must pray for courage to endure the scorn of the sophisticated world." *Supreme Court Justice Antonin Scalia (1999).* [34] Ibid. p. 137.

"Good Book and the spirit of the Savior have from the beginning been our guiding geniuses. Whether we look to the first Charter of Virginia, or to The Charter of New England, or The Charter of Massachusetts Bay or to The Fundamental Orders of Connecticut, the same objective is present...a Christian land governed by Christian principles...I like to believe we are living today in the spirit of the Christian religion." *Supreme Court Justice Earl Warren.* Ibid 138.

The secular humanist agenda is to keep the

Church in fear of the courts and the government. We have allowed a minority of atheists, championed by the ACLU, to make Christians believe that the government views them as second class citizens. However, there are more and more legal groups forming to meet and defeat the challenges of the ACLU.

Brad Bright, the son of Bill Bright the founder of Campus Crusade for Christ, has written a timely book titled *God Is the Issue*. He writes:

"The church in America today generally communicates with the culture in one of two ways. Either we preach the straight gospel without regard to the cultural and personal context, or we simply react defensively to the symptomatic cultural ills— such as homosexual behavior, abortion, racism, or pornography. Unlike Jesus, we have a difficult time using the cultural context as a relevant platform for making the God of the Bible the issue. Therefore, God comes across as largely irrelevant to the everyday life of the average American. Consequently, the culture ends up regarding us (along with the God of the Bible) as out of touch or, worse, dangerous." Brad Bright, *God Is the Issue*, (Peachtree City, GA: 2003): 16

Bright continues:

"The bottom line is this: we need a game plan that distinguishes between cause and effect. In that process, we need tactics that allow us to foil and frustrate the opposition by using their own tools and words against them—much like Jesus did with the Pharisees. It is time to return to the basics, but in a more culturally relevant and understandable manner." Ibid. p. 18.

Dr. Jerry Terrebrood

When Jesus encountered opposition from the Pharisees, He usually took what they already believed and put a new or proper perspective on it. How effective do we suppose He would have been, if He had retorted: *Anyone who would believe that is crazy!?*

All too often that has been the attitude of the Church, rather than cerebrally engaging with the culture, using the culture's own humanist belief system to make an appropriate counter analogy, the Church turns inwardly toward its own beliefs, and often with some dismissive quip, walks off the battlefield.

Deep within the air conditioned, gorgeously appointed sanctuary, seated in the padded pews, it is so easy to assume that one is a Christian Soldier; perhaps from the hymn just sung moments before.

I have often considered that the Church should be like a service station for automobiles. It is a place where we can get batteries recharged, fuel tanks refilled, and minor repairs to the wounds of life.

But, unlike the automobile, which is being refitted, refueled, and recharged, for service on the roads, Christians all too often leave the station only to park in a place with very little traffic. We should be out with spiritual jumper cables giving a charge to dead batteries, syphoning fuel from our tanks to share with others, pointing them to Christ's clinic for the healing of all manner of wounds. Yet, the atheists have informed us, that such is politically incorrect.

One can only conclude that if the Church spent

the same amount of time and effort studying its own day and time, as it does studying the times of yesteryear, the Church would be better equipped to engage in meaningful dialogue and educated debate that supports Christian belief.

Bright points out that we normally react to the effect and not the cause. By this he means that what the world is doing in their immoral lifestyles is demonstrating the effect of not having the proper causal agent in their life--God.

"The words of our second President, John Adams, are also profound:

'Our constitution was made only for a moral and religious people. It is wholly inadequate to the government of any other.'

If Washington and Adams were correct in their assessment, cultural conservatives need to take the next logical step in order to effectively turn the battle. We must become skilled at distinguishing between *cause* and *effect*. We must begin focusing more of our efforts on curing the disease instead of just treating the cultural symptoms. If we fail in this regard, it will be to our own detriment both as individuals and as a nation...Following the September 11th attacks on the World Trade Center and the Pentagon, some of our religious leaders laid the blame at the feet of the homosexuals, radical feminists, abortionists, pornographers, and other misguided groups of blind sheep. However on September 13, two days after the bombings, Jane Clayson of CBS's "The Early Show" interviewed Anne Graham Lotz, the daughter of Billy Graham. Jane asked her, 'If God is good, how could God, let this happen?' Anne's response nailed the cause dead center: 'For several years now Americans in a sense have shaken their fist at God and said, God, we want you out of our schools, our government, our business; we want you out of our marketplace. And God, who is a gentleman, has just quietly backed out of our national and political life, our public life, removing His hand of blessing and protection.'" Ibid. p. 23-4.

One is reminded by the foregoing of an often asked question when an airliner crashes and so many lives are lost: "How could a loving God let a thing like this happen?" Is the answer spiritual or is it physical?

Long before the invention of the airplane Newton discovered the principles of gravity.

It was not God who decided that man should defy these principles in a mechanical imitation of a bird. God did not say, "And thou shalt build unto thyself an aluminum tube and afix thereunto aluminum wings. Devise for thyself a form of power that shall thrust thee skyward whilst a great host resides inside the tube. And, thou shalt defy gravity for four hours or more from New York to L.A"

Man wants to be his, or her, own god, until things occur beyond man's ability to fix or solve, and then man wants to ask, "Why, if God loves man, would He let this happen?" Perhaps the reply should be, "If man is his own god, why did man let it happen?"

Chapter Five

A NATION OF REGULATIONS

II Corinthians 3:6
He has made us competent as ministers of a new
covenant—not of the letter but of the Spirit; for the letter kills,
but the Spirit gives life.
II Timothy 2:13-14
...If we died with him, we will also live with him; if we
endure, we will also reign with him. If we disown him, he will
also disown us; if we are faithless, he will remain faithful, for
he cannot disown himself. Keep reminding them of these
things. Warn them before God against quarreling about
words; it is of no value, and only ruins those who listen.

To begin; a quote from IRS Section 501(c) (3): "Under the Internal Revenue Code, all section 501(c)(3) organizations are absolutely prohibited from directly or indirectly participating in, or intervening in, any political campaign on behalf of (or in opposition to) any candidate for elective public office. Contributions to political campaign funds or public favor of or in opposition to any candidate for public office clearly violate the prohibition against political campaign activity. Violating this prohibition may result in denial or revocation of tax-exempt status and the imposition of certain excise taxes." The Restriction of Political Campaign Intervention by Section 501(c) (3) Tax Exempt Organizations:
www.irs.gov/charitites/charitable/article/O,,id+163385,00.html

Therefore, if Adolf Hitler, Attila the Hun, Genghis Khan, Joseph Stalin, or any other similar despot, were running for public office in this country, the Church may not speak out against them. The Church is allowed to encourage voting, but not to discuss the qualities, or lack thereof, concerning any candidate.

Does the Church need to face the facts? I see no way to sugar coat it. Is the Church being paid, by the government, through tax exemption, to sit back and be quiet?

Rev. D. James Kennedy remarked:

"The federal government has proved a tremendous impediment to the ongoing work of Christians. In all the laws that they have passed against Christian schools, gagging the church, taxation, and all kind of things that they have done, they have made it harder for the church to exercise its prerogatives and to preach the gospel...

Take the last presidential election. There were numbers of things that I knew that I was never able to say from the pulpit because if you advance the cause of one candidate or impede the cause of the other you can lose your tax exemption. That would have been disastrous not only for the church, but for our school and our seminary, everything. So you are gagged. You cannot do that. The IRS, a branch of our government, has succeeded in gagging Christians." Peter Kershaw, *Hushmoney*, (Branson, MO: Heal Our Land Ministries: 2011): 22

When court cases and legislation are being framed for introduction by the ACLU, and similar groups, we often find that the argument is about the wording of the constitution. The question for the court--sworn to defend the Constitution--is: What did the original writers intend? The court is not authorized to adapt the constitution to current views or practice, but that is often the result. The current trend is to legislate for, and to appeal to the courts for, "freedom *from* religion."

Was freedom from religion even in the thoughts of those who worded the Constitution?

Again we visit Wampler's insightful book concerning the foregoing:

"On November 7, 1801, the Baptists of Danbury, Connecticut, wrote Jefferson. They wondered if their religious exercise was a government-granted right rather than a God-granted right. They were worried that someday the government might try to regulate religious expression. Jefferson understood their concern. He assured them the free exercise of religion was an unalienable right which would not be meddled with by the government. He pointed out there was a 'wall of separation between church and state,' to ensure the government would never interfere with religious activities.

'Gentlemen,

The affectionate sentiments of esteem and approbation which you are so good as to express towards me, on behalf of the Danbury Baptist Association, gives me the highest satisfaction. My duties dictate a faithful and zealous pursuit of the interests of my constituents, and in the proportion as they are persuaded of my fidelity to those duties, the discharge of them becomes more and more pleasing.

Dr. Jerry Terrebrood

Believing with you that religion is a matter which lies solely between man and his God, that he owes account to none other for his faith, or his worship, that the legislative powers of government reach actions only, and not opinions, I contemplate with sovereign reverence that act of the whole American people which declared that their legislature should, '*make no law respecting an establishment of religion, or prohibiting the free exercise thereof*,' thus building a wall of separation between church and state'. . .

Since the birth of the Constitution, the *First Amendment* has been misunderstood and misquoted. Ask the average person on the street what it states and the vast majority will reply it says something about a 'wall of separation between church and state.'

Of course, that is not what it says at all. Jefferson's innocent, passing phrase has become, in the minds of perhaps most Americans, a substitute for the *First Amendment*, which spells out the role of religion in a Democratic Republic.

The *First Amendment* limits what Congress may do. It was written so that people would have full protection of their rights to free and unrestricted worship. But we have seen in our day a 180-degree turn from what the *First Amendment* says. Liberals and secular humanists proclaim that somehow the *First Amendment's* purpose is to protect the government from the influence of religion." Wampler, *The Myth of Separation Between Church and State,* 35&101.

The following is from Glenn Beck, a television commentator:

"After the signing of the Constitution, Benjamin Franklin was asked by a woman on the street, 'What have you given us, sir?' Franklin responded, 'A Republic, if you can keep it.'

A critical moment in history has come; our Republic is in jeopardy. Can we keep it?

If the answer to that question, as I fear, is 'no,' then we have no one to blame but ourselves. For too long we have ignored, enabled, or embraced the flawed character of those we've selected to protect and defend our Constitution. By lowering our standards for them, we've lowered the standards for ourselves. We wanted a life of ease, a life of little consequence and high reward. To get it, we repeatedly empowered thieves, liars, and con men, simply because they promised us ease. Now, because we've trained them that repeated injury has no consequence, they've grown bold and fearless. When we do speak up, they ease our pain with pork, a steady stream of entitlements, and financial candy, and back to sleep we go.

We have so little trust in the character of the people we elected that most of us wouldn't invite them into our homes for dinner, let alone leave our children alone their care. Yet we leave our children's financial future alone in their care. Why? Common sense tells us that this is national suicide."

Glenn Beck, *Glenn Beck's Common Sense*, (New York: Mercury Radio Arts, Inc.: 2009).

Obviously, Mr. Beck's focus, in this particular case, is upon the financial status of our country, but the sentiment is also true concerning the morality, the education, and the character of our nation. As the old saying goes, "You can't use the fox to guard the hen house."

Christians have sat back far too long and allowed the immoral, the indecent, the greedy, and the ungodly, to be voted into office. Partly because we are often ignorant of the issues, ignorant of the candidate's background, disinterested in, or repulsed by, the political process, or just too complacent to become involved.

The story is often told of a man and his wife who went to hear a motivational speaker. The speaker was driving home his point as follows: "The major problem in the country folks is ignorance and apathy, I tell you, ignorance and apathy!" The wife turned to her husband and whispered, "What do you think of that, Henry?" Henry replied, "I don't know and I don't care."

Perhaps many Christians are thinking: There's really nothing we can do. Many feel that the public is chained to the decisions and at the mercy of the courts, but Patrick J. Buchanan brings an interesting point in his book:

"Each time the Supreme Court hands down a decision without precedent in the law or the Constitution—outlawing school prayer or declaring abortion a right—conservatives demand that the Constitution be amended to overturn it. *This is the amendment trap, a fool's errand.* Any amendment must be approved by two-thirds of both houses of Congress and three-fourths of the state legislatures in seven years. *No truly controversial amendment has been enacted in our lifetime.* Invariably, the amendment is buried in committee as passions cool and the court decision is grudgingly accepted as the law of the land. Amendments on busing, flag burning, school prayer, abortion, and a balanced budget all perished this way. Is there recourse?

…There is a way. That is for Congress to use its Constitutional power to limit the jurisdiction of the Supreme Court and restore to the states the right to decide these matters.

In Article III, Section I, the Supreme Court is established and the Congress given power to 'ordain and establish' inferior courts. All U.S. courts, save the Supreme Court, are thus creations of Congress and can be abolished by Congress. And if Congress can abolish a court, it surely has the power to restrict the issues those courts may decide. And, that power is explicitly granted in Section II of Article III." Patrick J. Buchanan, *Where the Right Went Wrong*, (New York: St. Martin's Press: 2004) 227.

Each year more and more politically cognizant organizations are forming to present *amicus* briefs in support of the majority opinion concerning matters before the courts.

Some things for all Christians to consider are: Who are the recipients of our giving? What positive effect do they render with our offerings in the furtherance of the cause of Christ? Do the offerings go to the building of an earthly temple with a compound that isolates Christians from the world?

For example: The American Center for Law & Justice (ACLJ) is an organization with which I have no affiliation except as a monetary supporter of their work. There are other organizations as well, formed to represent us before the high courts. If we cannot go ourselves, it would seem wise to support those who go on our behalf.

Dr. Jerry Terrebrood

The world seems to have no difficulty raising funds to support immoral, indecent, and ungodly, causes. Surely, the Church militant needs to support the Army of the Lord in the battle against agents from the dark side.

Our own government can be dangerous to society by paying greater heed to minority voices and minority causes. We must remember that our own government was put in place by us, we the people. If then, this is a Christian nation, and we wish it to remain so, we cannot sit back and allow minority opinions, no matter how loudly proclaimed, or financially supported, to carry the day.

As stated above, if we cannot go ourselves, if few of us are capable of going before the courts then we have an obligation to seek and find the few who are capable, the few who are willing, and support them in "our" effort to put things back in a proper, moral, godly, perspective.

Some will say that we are living in the end times; the Bible states that the disappointing events we are witnessing were inevitable. "They" were saying that in Thessalonica in Paul's day (II Thessalonians chapter 2). "They" were saying that in 1949 when my folks were saved.

"They" have been saying it, and have been saying it, and one of these days "They" will be right. But, until that actual day, we cannot just take up space and "wait!" (pun intended).

Again, Jesus said, in Matthew's gospel chapter 11 and verse 12: "And from the days of John the Baptist until now the kingdom of heaven suffereth violence, and the violent take it by force" (KJV).

In Luke 22:25-36: "And he said unto them, When I sent you without purse, and scrip, and shoes, lacked ye anything? And they said, Nothing. Then He said unto them, But now, he that hath a purse, let him take it, and likewise his scrip: and he that hath no sword, let him sell his garment, and buy one" (KJV).

In today's vernacular Jesus may just as well have said, "Christianity is not for sissies!"

Are the words to the old hymn just words? "Onward Christian soldiers; marching as to war; with the cross of Jesus, going on before. Christ the royal Master leads against the foe; forward into battle, see His banners go!" We haven't always chosen our battles well nor defined our enemies properly.

Questions arise periodically: If this is a Christian nation, what kind of Christians do we mean? And, is there no place for Jews, Hindus, Muslims, Buddhists, et al?

Plainly the Bible reveals that the Jews persecuted the new sect of Christianity: And this, after Jews themselves had been persecuted by several other nations and persuasions.

Then Roman Catholicism, in the name of Christianity, came to the fore and persecuted any who were not of their persuasion. Many fled from Roman Catholic domination to Protestant England where they were persecuted for any belief other than Anglican. Many came to America where the Protestant pilgrims began persecuting one another: burning witches and heretics at the stake, all in

Christian love.

Then in America, Roman Catholics came for participation in the new world, and were promptly persecuted for being Roman Catholic. Mormons rose up in the nation and were persecuted by the traditional Christians. Jews came to America to escape the persecution in Europe and were promptly persecuted by the Protestant Christians, the Roman Catholics, and perhaps others, and so it goes, *ad nauseam, ad infinitum.*

When we review our history, is it any wonder that terms such as, "racism," "hate crimes," and "anti-defamation" have arisen. It was not Christianity, but rather the religions, that must share in the blame for much of our past—remembering that "religion" is often defined as how one puts into practice what one believes about God. We certainly did not get labels such as, bigots, accusers, elitists, etc., attached to us by only following the principles taught by Christ.

Religious freedom was the guarantee—not Christian religious sect exclusivity. Certainly we are entitled to vigorous debate concerning beliefs and doctrines. There is no provision or intention to stifle the processes of proselytization, no prohibition against differing viewpoints, and there was a full intent that no one religion could be forced upon the populace. However, when Christianity began persecuting others for their beliefs, we fell into the trap of trying to establish that ours was the "correct and therefore official" American religion. When The Constitution clearly states that there cannot be the establishment of any "state" religion.

Allowing other religions to practice their faith in a way that does not impinge upon the rights and safety of others is certainly within the precepts of the beatitudes, the Sermon on the Mount, and the U.S. Constitution. We should share what we believe, but not by force or coercion.

Thomas Jefferson wrote concerning religious liberty; in what became the Virginia Bill for Religious Liberty. His words are recorded by Peter A. Lilliback:

"Whereas Almighty God hath created the mind free; that all attempts to influence it by temporal punishments or burthens, or by civil incapacitations, tend only to beget habits of hypocrisy and meanness and are a departure from the plan of the Holy author of our religion, who being Lord both of body and mind, yet chose not to propagate it by coercions on either, as was in his almighty power to do.; that the impious presumption of legislators and rulers, civil as well as ecclesiastical, who being themselves but fallible and uninspired men, have assumed dominion over the faith of others, setting up their own opinions and modes of thinking as the only true and infallible, and as such endeavoring to impose them on others, that established and maintained false religions over the greatest part of the world, and through all time;... Be it enacted by the General Assembly, that no man shall be compelled to frequent or support any religious worship, place or ministry whatsoever, nor shall be enforced, restrained, molested, or burthened in his body or goods, nor shall otherwise suffer on account of his religious opinions or belief; but that all men shall be free to profess, and by argument to maintain, their opinion in matters of religion, and that the same shall in no wise diminish, enlarge, or affect their civil capacities." Peter Lilliback, *Wall of Misconception*, (West Conshohocken, PA: Providence Forum Press): 88-9.

Lillback continues with an account concerning Patrick Henry:

"Patrick Henry also had a significant impact on religious liberty in Virginia as well. In what became known as 'The Parson's Cause,' he helped defeat the required payment of tithes by the citizens of Virginia to the state church, a law that forced many to support a church they did not believe in. Henry also helped to defend persecuted preachers of the Gospel who were not part of the established church. William J. Federer writes, 'Prior to the Revolution, in 1768, Patrick Henry rode for miles on horseback to a trial in Spottsylvania County. He entered the rear of a courtroom where three Baptists ministers were being tried for having preached without the sanction of the Episcopalian Church. In the midst of the proceedings, he interrupted: *May it please your lordships, what did I hear read? Did I hear an expression that these men, who your worships are about to try for misdemeanor, are charged with preaching the gospel of the Son of God?* '" Ibid. p. 89-90.

There is a great difference between being religious and being Christian. Like the Pharisees in Jesus' day, there is danger in being too religious-- when form and formality replace Spirit and Grace.

How many denominations are there in America? Is it an indication of how many groups believe that they have the only true line on what is divine?

Jesus said, "All men shall know that you are my disciples, if you love one another" (John 13:35). "That they all may be one; as thou Father, art in me, and I in thee, that they also may be one in us: that the world may believe that thou has sent me...I in them and you in me. May they be brought to complete unity to let the world know that you sent me and have loved them even as you have loved me" (John 17:21 & 23).

Paul said, "I appeal to you brothers, in the name of our Lord Jesus Christ, that all of you agree with one another so that there may be no divisions among you and that you may be perfectly united in mind and thought." (I Cor. 1:10).

But, how does the world see us? They see us divided, arguing, bickering, disputing, defaming, and judgmental. It makes us hard to listen to when the world can't see past our noisy differences.

What is needed in reality will probably never happen. Jesus went to the cross and gave His life for people—even those who hated Him. Christians seem to have great difficulty being able to love and fellowship with each other—unless we're all in the same denomination. It isn't likely that the Church is going to suddenly appear to the world as a friendly, loving, place of refuge, accepting others just as they are.

Often I have wondered why, the Jewish people in particular, chosen of God, persecuted in so many lands, with such a religious heritage, could control an industry such as Hollywood, making such a mockery of God, and glorifying the worst in the carnal nature of man.

An interesting viewpoint by Orthodox Rabbi Daniel Lapin:

"Why do the descendants of the people who gave the world the Ten Commandments seem more hostile to them than anyone else in America? After a great deal of thought and years spent in detailed analyses of countless ancient Jewish texts that predict this trend in my people, the following is my answer. To understand this phenomenon, one has to know that Jewish attraction to liberalism is not new. In one form or another, many Jews have been liberals for more than three thousand years. Talmudic tradition reports that upon receiving the Ten Commandments, the Israelites wept. Their gloom was caused by the realization that the godly revelation they had just experienced now prohibited the lascivious lifestyle to which they had grown accustomed in Egypt. At that moment, liberalism was born: the eternal search for liberation from God's seemingly restrictive rules. There are those who will always seek—or if necessary, create—the escape hatch through which those who find God's rules too limiting can flee." Lilliback, *Walls of Misconception* p. 97.

Rarely do humans realize that the carnal nature of man is a bottomless and insatiable pit. There is no fleshly pleasure that can fill the void to the point that it will not always cry for more. The flesh will become dissatisfied with its last partaking and demand more and more; different and more; more thrilling; more dangerous; more prurient; more scintillating; Bigger, Better, More! More! More!

Until it has consumed the person like the cancer that it is; not unlike the black holes recently discovered in space. Because until man is regenerated, he has a void in his soul that only the Spirit of God can fill.

The world, the flesh, and the devil, will never love Christians. They will never accept us. They will never cease fighting against us. They will become ever more convinced that we are the actual cause of their misery. Nonetheless, we must fight on, in the streets, in the halls of government, in the courts.

We cannot isolate ourselves from the battlefield. Jesus died for the homosexuals, the addicts, the pornographers, the thief, the murderer, the child molester; He hates what they do, but He loves them. "God sent His Son, not to condemn the world but that the world through Him might be saved" (John 3:17). We are His voice, His hands, and His feet.

He commissioned us all to take the message to the far corners of the earth. We don't get to choose the battlefields; we wage the war wherever necessary. The war is made with love—not hate. The war is made with understanding—not judgment. The war is made with compassion—not rejection. The war is made by Christians—not religionists. The war is not waged by merely sitting in church.

Sam Kastensmidt writes:

"For decades, the American people have watched in frustration as the ACLU conspires with America's judiciary to eliminate religious expression from every conceivable state-sponsored venue—classrooms, graduations, football games, universities, local government meetings, state legislatures, congress, courtrooms, military academies, Christmas pageants, state-supported children's homes, and various faith-based initiatives.

Alan Sears, president of Alliance Defense Fund, explains:

'The ACLU desires a secular, faithless America where all memory of faith traditions and religion are absent from the public square, morals are relative, and where parental rights, religious freedom, and the sanctity of human life…are nearly non-existent. This is the America we will get unless we stand up to the ACLU.'" Sam Kastensmidt, *Indefensible; 10 ways the ACLU is destroying America*, (Coral Ridge, FL: Coral Ridge Ministries: 2006) 51.

We have examined writings of the founding fathers that demonstrate the nation and the Constitution were both founded upon the principles of a belief in God's providence and the right to religious freedom. Now, it is appropriate to consider that groups such as the ACLU have been effective in their attempts to erase everything about God from public education. But, let us review how higher education viewed this position when founded. From Lillback once again:

America's First Education Act:

"It being one chief purpose of that old deluder Satan, to keep men from the knowledge of the Scripture, it was therefore ordered that every township containing fifty families or householders should set up a school in which children might be taught to read and write, and that every township containing one hundred families or householders should set up a school in which boys might be fitted for entering Harvard College."

The Mottoes and Purpose Statements of America's Premier Colleges: *Harvard University* Motto: "*For Christ and the Church*" Established by Rev. John Harvard. 'First Fruits' in 1643: "After God had carried us safe to New England, and wee had builded our houses, provided necessaries for our livelihood, rear'd convenient places for Gods worship, and settled the Civil Government: Of the next things we longed for, and looked after was to advance Learning, and perpetuate it to Posterity, dreading to leave an illiterate Ministry to the churches, when our present Ministers shall lie in the Dust."

Rules and Precepts observed in the College: "Let every student be plainly instructed, and earnestly pressed to consider well, the main end of his life and studies is to know God and Jesus Christ which is eternal life, (John 17:3), and therefore to lay Christ in the bottom, as the only foundation of all sound knowledge and Learning."

College of William and Mary (Charter via Rev. James Blair) "To the end that the Church of Virginia may be furnished with a seminary of ministers of the gospel and…that the Christian faith may be propagated…to the glory of God

Y*ale University* (Official Charter 1701) "For the liberal and religious education of suitable youth…to propagate in this wilderness, the blessed reformed Protestant religion."

Princeton University

Dr. Jerry Terrebrood

First President, Rev. Jonathan Dickinson: "Cursed be all that learning that is contrary to the cross of Christ." Official Motto: "Under God's Power She Flourishes."

Rutgers University Official Motto: "Son of Righteousness, Shine upon the West also." Lilliback, *Walls of Misconception*, 104-5.

It becomes patently obvious that the founding fathers had no intention whatsoever of removing Christian education from the schools, nor removing the mention of God, prayer to God, or any such foolishness as has been interpreted and ruled in modern days.

The United States is becoming a far more immoral nation as each year passes. A major force behind the manipulation and secularization of the court system has been the ACLU. There is no nice way to say it: The ACLU supports evil. The following excerpt from a book written by Alan Sears and Craig Osten is revealing. The narrative concerns the kidnapping, abuse, and murder of a ten year old boy named Jeffrey Curley of Cambridge, Mass. I will refrain from the sordid details and begin with a brief summary. The men, Sicari and Jaynes, were subscribers to a Website called The North American Man/Boy Love Association (NAMBLA):

"Sicari and Jaynes were caught and eventually convicted for their wicked crimes. They now are serving life imprisonment. (Jeffrey's parents) filed a $200 million civil lawsuit against NAMBLA, claiming that their son might still be alive if not for the "man-boy love" organization and the content of its 'educational' Web site...The ACLU came to

NAMBLA's defense, against the protection of young boys like Jeffery Curley.

Incredibly, the ACLU's Massachusetts executive director, John Roberts, said, 'There was nothing in those publications (of NAMBLA) or Web site which advocated or incited the commission of any illegal acts, including murder or rape...'

To most people, Web pages that provide advice on how to seduce and rape young boys would be enough evidence for a civil lawsuit that NAMBLA is encouraging and inducing its members to engage in lawless action. However, this does not seem to matter in the eyes of the ACLU." Alan Sears and Craig Osten; *The ACLU vs AMERICA.* (Nashville: Broadman & Holman Publishers, 2005): 75-6).

Much was left out of the foregoing because of the fact that it was of a nauseating nature. There are many, many, similar cases cited in the book, but this one should be sufficient to make the point.

The ACLU and other similar organizations are atheistic, immoral, indecent, blights on society. How long will it be? How much will it take before the Christian world throws itself into the war with dollars and votes to stem the tide of evil that is infecting our nation? The Church is not immune. This conduct happens within the church body to one degree or another: Child molestations, pornography, homosexual behavior, etc. We need to hear the cry from the pulpits: ENOUGH!!!!!!!!!!!!!

When will the Church find the courage to stand up and shout that sin is still sin!? When will the Church tell the IRS to keep their tax exempt conditions? Do we have enough Christian Soldier left in us to speak against sin, anytime, anywhere, refusing to be silenced? Hating what people do *is not* the same as hating them. We know that our past U.S. President, George Bush, was a Christian and was open about it.

Former President Bill Clinton is quoted in Jay Alan Sekulow's book:

"...before high school students in Virginia, President Bill Clinton came out in favor of religious speech in our nation's public schools. He emphasized the need for us to continue to be a nation of toleration for the beliefs of others. He also discussed the need for us to no longer disqualify students simply because of their religious beliefs. President Clinton specifically addressed the rights of students to express their beliefs on campus. He stated that students have the right to 'pray privately and individual whenever they want. The can say grace themselves before lunch. There are times when they can pray out loud together. Student religious clubs in high schools can and should be treated just like any other extracurricular club. They can advertise their meetings, meet on school grounds, and use school facilities, just as other clubs can. When students choose to read a book (silently) to themselves, they have every right to read the Bible or any other religious text they want.'...He declared the need for the government to protect the rights of students by noting that, 'some student religious groups haven't been allowed to publicize their meetings, in the same way that nonreligious groups can. Some students have been prevented even from saying grace before lunch.' The President then offered solutions to the problem of religious discrimination. 'Wherever and whenever the religious rights of children are threatened or suppressed we must move quickly to correct it. We want to make it easier and more acceptable for people to express and to celebrate their faith.'

President Clinton has even given the Justice Department guidelines for implementing his stated religious rights on public school campuses. The heart of the President's speech is summed up in this one statement taken from the speech: 'This country needs to be a place where religion grows and flourishes.'" Jay Alan Sekulow, *The Christian The Court and The Constitution*, (Virginia Beach; The American Center for Law and Justice: 2000): 70-1.

Christians need to remain abreast of these things. The liberal media will always make, if they can, even the most mundane item sound or read like some sensational event has occurred. The Church needs to be aware of legislation, court rulings, civic occurrences, and not be intimidated by those with special interests who try, as Satan does, to instill fear in the believers. We need to put our money, our minds, and our votes on things and in places where it counts most for the cause of Christ and the freedoms granted to us by the Constitution.

PART III

ISLAM: FRIEND OR FOE?

Do not be yoked together with unbelievers. For what does righteousness and wickedness have in common? Or what fellowship can light have with darkness? What harmony is there between Christ and Belial? What does a believer have in common with an unbeliever? (II Cor. 6:14-15)

In the United States, there has historically been a welcoming of immigrants from foreign lands. These immigrants bring with them the culture, the language, and the religions of their former countries. The general populace has usually been more welcoming to those with different backgrounds, customs, and beliefs than has been the case for religions toward one another.

As previously discussed, we need only look at

the significant number of different denominations within Christianity to see this trend towards exclusivity. We have divided ourselves into many camps predicated upon differing views of the same subject—each camp content in the belief that they have the correct views. A visitor to the camp is not unwelcome insofar as he or she does not wish to question the party line.

We all read from the same book—accepting that there are various versions of the book. Many of the camps hold strong opinions about a particular version being the only true version of the book.

In some camps the service is conducted in such a manner that one would think him or herself to be attending a "rock concert." That term may be an oxymoron based on the requirement of satisfying the meaning of "concert" and its dependence upon harmony and togetherness. But, I press on.

In other services, one might think that a funeral is being held, but there is no obvious casket at the front. There are variations of everything in between. Ironically, it is religious freedom in action—guaranteed by the Constitution.

Thus when another religion appears, from within the U.S. e.g., Universalists; Mormons; Wiccans; Satanists; Jehovah's Witnesses; etc., we are gracious and afford them the same freedoms that we enjoy—this is America.

When other religions arrive on our shores as a part of immigration, e.g. Jews; Buddhists; Hindus; Islam; etc., we are gracious and afford them the same freedoms that we enjoy—this is America.

However, there is a difference between

religious tolerance and submitting to victimization through religious deception. Our Constitution guarantees religious freedom as long as the religion abides by the laws of our country and does no harm to society.

Islam is an example of a religion with an agenda that differs from the other religions. Nearly all religions will accept new converts. Most have some form of proselytization. Christians often speak of "Winning the world for Christ." However, Islam preaches a religious goal of forcing the world to accept Islam.

Some, unwittingly, call Islam a religion of peace. But, the underlying documents of the faith, the Quran and Hadiths, and the history of the religion, tell a different story.

History reveals that Islam has lived in peace with other religions when Islam was not in the majority or in a dominant military position. However, when Islam is in the majority, whether by population, or force of arms, they only live in peace, if the dominated religions are willing to pay them tribute money, and live under Islamic law. If the dominated were unwilling to pay the tribute, and/or would not convert to Islam, they were put to humiliation and the sword.

This treatise will not be a comparison/contrast of the theological views of Islam and Christianity— there are many books for reference on that subject. I will concentrate my efforts on examining whether there can be harmony between Islam and Christianity.

Certainly Christianity will expend considerable

efforts in converting Muslims from Islam to Christianity and Islam will attempt the reverse. This exploration will consider whether this can be done peacefully, or will it bring forth a schism that may erupt into violence and murder as it has traditionally done in other countries. It surfaced significantly in our country on September 11, 2001.

This chapter will ask, and attempt to answer, eight questions:

1. Who was Muhammad?
2. How did the Quran come to be?
3. What was the first incident that set Muhammad against Christians and Jews?
4. When did Islam rise to power and how long were they dominant?
5. What was the second incident that set Islam against Christians and Jews?
6. What is Militant Islam?
7. What is "Chrislam?"
8. Is the nation of Israel actually in jeopardy from Islam?

Who was Muhammad?

First, let us wonder whether there ever really was a Muhammed as described by the believers of Islam. The task of presenting the evidences for Muhammed's existence or non-existence is beyond the scope of this treatise. Herein, I present what the Muslims believe and have said concerning him.

Sometimes attempting to prove that something exists or existed is an extremely difficult task. However, trying to prove that something never existed is impossible. Keeping that in mind, I would refer the reader to Robert Spencer's NYT best seller *Did Muhammed Exist?* Published by the Intercollegiate Studies Institute (ISI books) 2012. It is an excellent examination of the evidences or lack thereof for Muhammed actually having existed during the time frame claimed for him.

"According to tradition, Muhammad was born in Mecca on April 20, A.D. 570: (or April 26 according to Shi'ites). Tradition holds his father died soon after he was born and his mother died when he was only six; before that, he had been entrusted to a foster mother and nursemaid, as was customary...The chain of events that would make him the leader and inspiration of all *jihads* was set in motion when he met a distant cousin, Khadija bint Khywaylid, whom Ibn Ishaq calls "a merchant woman of dignity and wealth." ...fifteen years older than Muhammad, she was a woman of significant accomplishment when they met. She hired him as a traveling salesman to go to Syria and trade her goods...impressed that Muhammad had doubled her wealth on his journey she proposed marriage, although she was forty and Muhammad just twenty-five." Robert Spencer, *The Truth About Muhammad; founder of the world's most intolerant religion.* (Washington, D.C. Regnery Publishing, Inc. 2001): 35-8.

There is a document within the sacred writing of Islam called the *Hadith*. This is primarily a collection of personal recollections written by those who claim to have actually come in contact with Muhammad, and who knew some particular story or event, or an explanation of some event and how Quranic verses apply.

Within the *Hadith* the stories are accumulated

according to a particular school of thought, e.g. *Bukhari* or *Muslim*. There is evidence among these writings that provide evidence that Muhammad may have been a white man:

(a) Bukhari:3.47.769;5.59.612;
       8.75.392; 9.86.108; 9.89.286

(b) Muslim: 20.4509; 20.4511

Each of the documents listed above tell of an instance wherein Muhammad raised his arms in praise or prayer and the narrator describes that Muhammad raised his hands so high that the **whiteness** of his armpits could be seen.

(c) Bukhari 1.3.63: "While we were sitting with the Prophet in the mosque, a man came, riding on a camel. He made his camel kneel down in the mosque, tied its foreleg and then said: 'Who amongst you is Muhammad?' At that time the Prophet was sitting amongst us (his companions) leaning on his arm. We replied, 'this white man reclining on his arm.'"

(d) Bukhari 1.8.367: "The Prophet passed through the lane of *Khaibar* quickly and my knee was touching the thigh of the Prophet. He uncovered his thigh and I saw the whiteness of the thigh of the Prophet."

(e) Muslim 4.1014: "Then the Apostle of Allah (may peace be upon him) stepped out with a red mantle on him and I was catching a glimpse of the whiteness of his shanks." [52] (a) through (e): www.quranexplorer.com/hadith/english/Hadith/Muslim.html

It would seem obvious that unless the sight of that whiteness was considered as something unusual, it would not have been noted and recorded so many times.

How did the Quran come to be?

It is generally believed by Muslims that Muhammad claimed to have been visited by the Angel Gabriel, who commanded him to memorize and recite what Gabriel gave him to read--Although, in Muhammad's version of the event, he could not read. However, for the next 23 years, until his death, Muhammad would recite for his followers the things he was supposedly told by Gabriel. His followers, according to Islamic tradition, committed them to memory and later wrote them on whatever was available. This was what became known as the **Quran** (Koran).

"Soon after Muhammad's death in 632, a handful of Arabian tribes declared their independence from the Islamic community. Abu Bakr, Muhammad's successor, sent an army to subjugate them in what became known as the battle of **Yamama**. There, a significant number of Muhammad's companions, who knew large portions of his recitations, died in battle. Indeed, one of those killed was Salim, the freed slave of Abu Hudhaifa, whom Muhammad had named as one of the four best reciters of the Koran. Abu Bakr realized that words of Muhammad might die out with the demise of that first generation of converts.

The man whom Abu Bakr commissioned to recover, record, and print in one authoritative document was Zaid ibn Thabit. An excerpt from the story, narrated by Zaid himself is told as follows, taken from al-Bukhari 6:509 (the *Hadith*):

"...Abu Bakr kept on urging me to accept his idea until Allah opened my chest for what He had opened the chests of Abu Bakr and Umar. So I started looking for the Qur'an and collecting it from palm stalks, thin white stones and also from the men who knew it by heart, till I found the last verse of Surat At-Tauba (repentance) with Abi Khuzaima Al-Ansari, and I did not find it with anybody other than him...Then the complete manuscripts of the Qur'an remained with Abu Bakr till he died, then with Umar till the end of his life, and then with Hafsa, the daughter of Umar." Mateen Elass, *Understanding the Koran*, (Grand Rapids: 2004): 41-2.

This writing in the Hadith contradicts the popular Muslim belief that the entire Qur'an had been unerringly memorized by a number of Muhammad's followers whose versions all coincided. Zaid records that he searched through many sources and decided the process was complete only when he discovered the last verse, which only one person had. There were already reports of varying versions of the sayings being used in different places, and other efforts were underway at the same time, to compile their own versions of the complete text.

Throughout history, the Muslims have defended the transmission as being directly from Muhammad to the reciters, without interruption.

When the Koran refers to passages or stories in the Bible, it often differs with the Biblical text. When these errors were called to the attention of Muhammad, his "revelations" would state that the Jews and Christians were once delivered a perfect document, but they intentionally corrupted it. The

Muslims continue that line of argument to this day.

Often Muhammad would give a revelation and then at some later date give one that contradicted it. He would explain this usually in one of two ways:

(1) God made a mistake on the first one, or changed His mind, and gave a better one

(2) Muhammad's memory was incorrect and the new one corrected his mistakes.

This is often referred to as the rule of abrogation. It is also employed by Mormons concerning differing revelations supposedly given to the Mormon prophet.

What was the first incident that set Islam against Christians and Jews?

"In the early years at medina there were two important developments. Muhammad had been greatly excited by the prospect of working closely with the Jewish tribes, and had even, shortly before the *hijrah,* introduced some practices (such as communal prayer on Friday afternoons, when Jews would be preparing for the Sabbath, and a fast on the Jewish Day of Atonement) to align Islam more closely with Judaism. His disappointment, when the Jews of medina refused to accept him as an authentic prophet, was one of the greatest of his life. For Jews, the era of prophecy was over, so it was not surprising that they could not accept Muhammad, but the polemic with the Jews of Medina occupies a significant proportion of the Quran and shows that it troubled Muhammad.

By A.D. 624 it was clear that most of the Jews of Medina would never be reconciled with the

Prophet. Muhammad had also been shocked to learn that the Jews and Christians (whom he had assumed to belong to a single faith) actually had serious theological differences, even though he appears to have thought that not all the *abl al-kitab* condoned this disgraceful sectarianism. In January A.D. 624, he made what must have been one of his most creative gestures. During the *salat* prayer, he told the congregation to turn around, so that they prayed in the direction of Mecca rather than Jerusalem." Karen Armstrong, *ISLAM; a short history*; (New York: Modern Library, 2002): 17-8.

Perhaps an explanation of why Mecca is of such important to Muslims is in order. In Mecca, there is a building called the *Kabah*, which is Arabic for "cube." It is the belief of Islam that this building was originally built by Adam and Eve. Over the centuries it fell into disrepair. When Hagar and Ishmael were sent away at the behest of Sarah, (Genesis 21:10-20) the Muslims believe they settled in Mecca and that Abraham came to visit them. They believe that Abraham and Ishmael rebuilt the *Kabah*.

It is said to be built around a large black stone. The Muslims make a pilgrimage to Mecca and there they pass around this stone touching it while they pray. The legend is that the stone was originally white, but the sins of the pilgrims who have touched it over the centuries have turned it black.

When did Islam rise to power and how long were they dominant?

"The outward expansion by Muslims began in earnest around A.D. 625 In the 23 years of

Dr. Jerry Terrebrood

Muhammad's rise to prominence he had managed to subdue and subject the entire Arabian Peninsula. He died in A.D. 632. Islam broke out of the confines of the Arabian Peninsula and headed north and west.

Only ten years after Muhammad's death Alexandria and all of Egypt were in the hands of the Muslims. The church in Egypt greeted them with mixed feelings: because of its one-nature doctrine about Jesus, they had been treated roughly, as little better than heretics, by the rest of the churches that accepted the Chalcedonian doctrine of the two natures of Jesus, human and divine. The Muslims treated them rather better than the byzantine Christians had done.

The Muslim advance across North Africa continued: in another fifty years Carthage fell, and the whole of North Africa was theirs. The Berbers needed little persuasion to accept Islam: their language was, after all, related to Arabic and not at all to Greek or Latin. ...While some converts had been made among them, most of the Berbers seem to have remained non-Christian.

The Muslim advance proceeded further, now strengthened by the accession of the Berbers. One of them, Tarik, led the leap across the Mediterranean to Gibraltar and even gave it the name Jabal Tarik.

There is a lesson there for the church to learn: when it buries its head in monasteries and libraries, when it concerns itself primarily with philosophy and abstract theology, when it loses sight of the people, the consequences for both church and people are likely to be catastrophic." Peter G. Riddell and Peter Cotterell, *Islam in Context; past, present, and future*, (Grand Rapids: Baker Academic: 2003): 70-1.

The Crusades began in the years between A.D.1000 and 1100. History varies concerning the events of the Crusades, it is told differently by the Crusaders who called themselves "pilgrims" compared to the events as told by the Muslims, who the Crusaders referred to as "pagans." The Crusades ended in A.D. 1291

The country of Spain was under Muslim control until the middle of the eleventh century. When the Muslims entered France they were defeated and their advance halted. It required multiple efforts to expunge the Muslims from Spain, and their final stronghold in Granada was conquered in January 1492. There was a resurgence of Muslim advance by the Ottoman, Turks who conquered all the way to Vienna and were defeated by the King of Poland's armies on September 11, 1683.

Distrust and persecutions were the normal order of things among Jews, Christians and Muslims for years to come.

For centuries, the Arabic countries exceled in scholarship, craftsmanship, and science. As the West became industrialized, the Muslim nations did not, and the tide of progress swept them away, and when combined with their penchant for clinging to an Islamic philosophy of life that kept them in their antiquated ways, they were left far behind the social progress of the West.

They found themselves horribly behind in an

advancing technology. When the world was flying aircraft, driving automobiles, and fighting wars with machines, the Muslim countries were still riding horses and camels, watching as aircraft flew overhead, and fighting with ancient weapons. They could no longer compete.

But, the pot was soon to begin rising to the boil.

What was the second incident that set Islam against Christians and Jews?

"During the course of World War I, the British government—strongly influenced by (James) Balfour, then foreign secretary—became convinced that its support of a Zionist program in Palestine would not only be a humanitarian gesture but would also serve British Imperial interests in the Middle East. Thus in November 1917 Britain issued the ***Balfour Declaration*** which stated:

"His majesty's Government view with favour the establishment in Palestine of a national home for the Jewish people, and will use their best endeavors to facilitate the achievement of this object, it being clearly understood that nothing shall be done which may prejudices the civil and religious rights of existing non-Jewish communities in Palestine..."

Between the two world wars, Palestine was the most tempestuous area in all the Middle East, as Britain sought to protect its imperial interests and at the same time reconcile them with Zionism and Arab nationalism. Almost as soon as the mandate was set up, Arab riots broke out in Palestine. In 1919 the population was given at 700,000, with

568,000 Arabs, 58,000 Jews, and 74,000 others, mainly Christians…the fact that Jewish immigration was not large made possible a period of peace and progress from 1922 to 1929. As Zionists reclaimed land, set up collective farms, harnessed the Jordan for power, and established many new factories, a veritable economic revolution took place. Tel-Aviv grew into a thriving modern city, an excellent university was founded at Jerusalem, and Palestine became the center of a Hebrew renaissance.

The era of peace ended in 1929 when serious disorders broke out, mainly Arab attacks on Jews. Violence continued to erupt in the early 1930's as the Nazi persecution of the Jews brought about a steep rise in immigration to Palestine and threatened the Arabs' predominant position in the area. In 1937 a British commission of inquiry recommended a tripartite division: Palestine would be divided into two independent states, one controlled by the Arabs and one by the Jews, with Britain holding a third portion, a small mandated area containing Jerusalem and Bethlehem. This recommendation satisfied no one and was not accepted.

Throughout the 1930's the "Palestine Question" was violently discussed in many parts of the world. Zionists argued that they had a historic right to the holy Land, their original home, that Palestine had been promised to them in the *Balfour Declaration* and legalized by the League of Nations, that Jewish colonization constituted a democratic and progressive influence in the Middle East; and that Arab antipathy was mainly the work of a few wealthy effendis, since the mass of Arabs were profiting from the wealth being brought into Palestine. On the other hand, the Arabs argued that Palestine had been their country for more than a thousand years and declared that the Balfour Declaration did not bind them because they were not consulted in its formulation." T. Walter Wallbank, Alastair M. Taylor, Nels M. Bailkey, and George F. Jewsbury, *Civilization Past and Present, single volume-fifth edition-special printing*, (Glenview, IL. Scott, Foresman and Company: 1983): 734-5.

Of course we know that today Israel is surrounded by her enemies, nearly all of them Muslim. Many prognosticators of Biblical eschatology believe that the Battle of Armageddon will be the result of a final assault by Russia in league with the Muslim Middle-East coming against Israel.

What is Militant Islam

According to the foregoing, it would seem that this question needs very little explanation. However, there are many underlying issues that need to be addressed. The Church and the media are being led to believe that there are at least two, separate and different factions within Islam. There are indeed two major sects among the Muslims: Shi'ites and Sunnis. The press would tend to describe the Sunnis as more westernized, moderate, and peaceful; whereas the Shi'ites are described as, separatist, fundamentalist, terrorists. There is truth in that analogy, but it is naïve for the Government, or the Church, to believe that Sunnis are just "good ole boys" trying to get along with everyone. Their history, their literature, and their belief systems speak for themselves. The Islamic force behind ISIS is Sunni.

We have already discussed the unrest in Palestine beginning in the early 1900's and continuing until this day. The 1900's began the age of industrialization, particularly in the West. This brought a need for an expendable commodity—oil. Britain, France, Germany, and Holland were rapidly advancing as well as the United States.

In the early going, the United States had discovered its own oil supplies within the continental U.S.

Britain, France, Germany, and Holland, had to go elsewhere for the river of crude oil it would take to feed their industrial advance. The middle-east was a ready source of their need for oil. Each country was staking their claims in the middle-east as well as Africa.

Saudi Arabia is an oil rich region, but in the early 1900's was under the control of the Turks. Britain, with an eye on the oil reserves in Saudi Arabia, began to assist the Arabs with weapons and advice, including the famed Lawrence of Arabia, in their efforts to gain independence from Turkey. The cost to the Arabs of course, was to allow British petroleum developers to aid the Saudi's in the development of their oil fields.

The idea caught on and soon the French and the Dutch were actively engaged in countries in the middle-east to assist them in developing their oil reserves.

Germany was gearing up for war and they too needed the oil rich supplies of the middle-east.

Dr. Jerry Terrebrood

During World War I, while the industrialized nations farmed, traveled, and made war with machines, the middle-east still farmed, traveled, and made war riding upon animals. It didn't take them long to catch on and begin to want to catch up.

Soon the middle-eastern countries began to nationalize the oil fields, taking control of production and pricing. They began to be the recipients of the wealth instead of watching it all go into the hands of foreigners.

At the end of World War II, there were many arms manufacturers who had been dependent upon the warring governments as a market. When this market dried up, they began to find ready markets in the middle-east for their weapons. Oil allowed the middle-east to begin to flourish economically, but weapons began to be the catalyst for Muslim fundamentalism to flourish.

As the morals of the West began to decay, and Movies, TV, and the Internet, began to be in even some of the most remote parts of the world, the Muslim Fundamentalist movement began to do what the Christian West had failed to do: they rose up in defiant and indignant protest.

Of course, they fail to recognize the atrocities they commit, in the name of Allah and according to the Koran and Sharia law, are far worse than decayed morals concerning human relations.

There are many geo-political issues that led to the attack on the twin towers in 2001, and they are beyond the scope of this book. Therefore, I restrict myself, from this point on, to issues that I feel are pertinent to the dangers of Islam where Christianity is concerned.

We begin with a look at the Christian Church as compared to Islam. The following is a lengthy excerpt:

"The non-Muslim world's secular value systems, as well as its religious institutions, (has) waned in authority while Islam's reach in the world, and Islam's violence in its name, (have) increased. Catholicism's internal moral disorders, for instance, reduced even wealthy American dioceses to bankruptcy in lawsuits brought against them for the crimes and delinquencies of God's ostensible servants, and led to the resignations not only of American Bishops, but of bishops from Austria to Argentina and from Canada to Poland. For many, these disorders—found on a lesser scale in Anglicanism also—compromised Christianity itself; even if Christian evangelism, especially in Africa and Latin America grew stronger in the contest of faiths, or new wars of religion.

Many seminaries, monasteries, convents and churches closed in Western Europe and North America—despite the religious vitality of Hispanic Catholic immigrants to the United States—while the number of mosques grew; in Britain, for example, mosques sometimes took over vacated church buildings. Some three thousand Catholic schools also closed in the US in the four decades from the 1960s, while the Church of England lost half its membership in thirty years. In many countries outside the 'developing' world, callings to the Catholic priesthood fell, in some cases—as in Britain and Ireland—precipitously, while Imams entered Europe in increasing numbers to attend to, and in a minority of cases to incite, their faithful. Only one priest was ordained in Dublin in 2002, and eight in Ireland, and only a mere eighteen in the whole of England and Wales in 2004. In 1965, one in thirty Catholic parishes in the U.S. had no resident priest; by 2002, it was one in six...In April 2002, the Church of Scotland itself predicted that it would become extinct within 50 years at its current rate of decline and fewer than 3 per cent of Londoners were said in 2004 to be regular churchgoers. Even in Spain, where half a century ago 98 per cent declared themselves to be practicing Catholics, only 18 per cent did so in 2004.

'Europe is no longer Christian' the general-secretary of the United Reform Church in Britain asserted in June 2003. 'I would be hard pushed to say we were a Christian country', similarly declared the archbishop of York in December 2004; in a British poll published in March 2005, less than half of the respondents knew why Christians celebrate Easter...

The Muslim nation-state of course exists, including in the most repressive forms. But there is no concept of the political state as such in the Koran whose teachings are universal in their scope.

Pious, as well as many 'ordinary,' Muslims hold that an Islamic nation is a religious state before it is a political entity, and as such part of an Islamic world community whose interests transcend those of a mere state... Hence, the Muslim...who seeks 'Islamist rule on earth', and who carries Holy Writ (he believes) in one hand and a weapon in the other (believes) all geographical boundaries—and moral limits when occasion demands—can be crossed when the common fate of Muslims is felt to be at stake." David Selbourne, *The Losing Battle With Islam,* (Amherst, NY: Prometheus Books 2005): 478-9. (comments in parenthesis mine)

The Christian Church needs to wake up. In my geographical area there are probably 100 churches that will seat more than 100 people. Many have difficulty gathering more than 25 attendees on a Sunday morning. Many have canceled the mid-week and the Sunday evening services, because people will not support them. Multiple reasons for this sad result are given. One of the major reasons is the aging of the congregations, which was addressed in the Secular Humanism portion of this document.

Muslims, at their base, are fanatical. They will kill non-believers; and this includes other Muslims who disagree with their fundamentalist dogma.

Where Christianity has difficulty maintaining relevance to the age group from 14 to 35, Muslims teach their children fanaticism in the schools, in the Mosque, and by the time they become teenagers, they are well indoctrinated and staunch believers in their cause. In other words, however much we may disagree with what they believe and how they carry out their beliefs--they do what they do better than we do what we do.

History reveals in many sources, the Koran itself, and the Hadith, that Muhammad's approach to non-believers was three fold: (1) Accept that there is no God but Allah; (2) Confess that Muhammad is Allah's prophet; and that all the earth belongs to Allah and Allah's prophet. Failing to do so, required the Muslims to fight you until you do, or (3) pay Islam a life-time tribute to let you live. It was his primary source of funding other than caravan raiding and plundering the cities of the infidels.

How do they plan to bring about their agenda in the U.S.? Hitler said words to the effect: *Give me the children and in ten years I'll change German society.*

According to a speech given by Bridgette Gabriel, the founder of ACT America, the oil rich middle-east, for years, has been pumping millions of dollars into our colleges and universities to 'develop' middle-east departments of study. I would say: in order to plant propaganda.

We send High School students to college and many of them return to us with a hatred for the country they were born in. The Saudis in particular have been working this agenda for years. They donate the money to the University to establish the department; then they have influence, if not control, over the curriculum, and the hiring of the faculty.

The following is an excerpt from a newsletter from Christians United for Israel (CUFI) dated 4/21/2015:

"There is a dark (Palestinian led) effort underway to Boycott, Divest from and Sanction (BDS) the Jewish state of Israel. The heart of this effort is found on America's college campuses. The leaders of this movement have no interest in seeing the Jewish state live in peace with her neighbors. They have but one goal: Destroy the Jewish state through international isolation.

The tactics associated with BDS are nothing short of appalling. They demonize the Jewish state. They lie about the actions of the Israeli government. And they bully and intimidate pro-Israel students.

Since the BDS movement first reared its ugly head about ten years ago it has gained momentum on college campuses across the country. In the last few years, this obscene effort to single out Israel for economic punishment has won a string of victories in California. Just last month, Northwestern and Stanford Universities both voted in favor of divesting from Israel..."

Again, according to Ms. Gabriel, Muslims have also gotten together with the publishing companies, e.g. McGraw-Hill, Houghton-Mifflin, Macmillan, Harper and Row, etc. influencing them on how Islam should be portrayed to our students in social studies classes.

During her speech in Nashville, at an Anti-Sharia conference, videoed and published by T*he Tennessean,* she produced a copy of a grade school course titled: *ISLAM.* Money has always been able to purchase influence in government and education.

In the typical American home, the Dad can tell you more about who is playing for a professional sports team than what his children are being taught at school. The Mom knows the characters she likes on her favorite TV shows, but may not have a clue as to what her children are being taught.

Many public school teachers are aware of these things, but, job security demands a low profile and no waves made.

Dr. Jerry Terrebrood

Muslims have begun using against us what they see as weaknesses in our system of laws. Following the lead of many minority voices before them, they are lobbying for laws to be enacted or changed to benefit the advancement and the advantage of Islam in our country.

As previously mentioned, organizations such as the American Center for Law & Justice (ACLJ) monitor these cases, and prepare amicus briefs to present to the court on issues. However, unless there is a much greater emphasis placed on these issues, the American public will be undermined by Saudi oil money and influence. Stephen Schwartz states the following:

"In the aftermath of September 11, the Saudi authorities were asked, as allies of the United States in the anti-terror war, to investigate, freeze, and seize the bank accounts of participants in and contributors to terrorist activities. In addition, like other foreign carriers, Saudi airlines were asked to provide advance passenger lists for flights to the United States. These requests were not specifically prompted by the discovery that 15 out of the 19 terrorists involved in the attacks on New York and Washington were Saudi citizens and the long-standing awareness that most of Osama bin Laden's funds also came from the kingdom. Rather, they were viewed as almost perfunctory measures necessary for a refused compliance…

The Saudi Embassy's official Web site in Washington turned out to have advertised the outlay of hundreds of millions of dollars for the families of 'martyrs,' i.e., suicide terrorists, in Israel. A Saudi telethon collected $109 million more for the 'martyrs' in April 2002.

The Wahhabi cleric who hosted the telethon, Shaykh Saad al-Buraik, preached in a mosque in Riyadh, calling for the enslavement of the Jewish women of Israel, once Palestinian victory was achieved.

Referring to Jews as 'monkeys,' al-Buraik declared, 'Muslim brothers in Palestine do not have mercy or compassion toward the Jews, their blood, their money, or their flesh. Their women are yours to take, legitimately. God made them yours. Why don't you enslave their women? Why don't you wage jihad? Why don't you pillage them?' Stephen Schwartz;*The Two Faces of Islam*, (NY: Anchor Books:2003: 276-7).

Yet, for reasons unknown, the U.S. Government has counted Saudi Arabia as an ally. Muslims in America would overthrow us by force if they could. Since they cannot, they have three items in their agenda: immigration; reproduction; and conversion. Overwhelming the country with immigrants might produce a backlash and reproduction will take a long time. Therefore, they saw converting Americans to Islam as the central focus of Muslims in the U.S.

However, recent floods of Muslim immigrants to the United States has increased the emphasis on immigration and reproduction. It has been reported that the average birth rate for U.S. families is slightly less than 2 children per year. Whereas among Muslims the number is slightly over 5 per year.

It is commonly reported in many histories of Islam, concerning Muhammad, that he and his followers, captured, kept, and sold members of the black race as slaves. In so doing, in Africa and Ethiopia, they made converts to Islam. The converted Africans and Ethiopians then began to hunt and capture other members of their country to be sold in the Muslim slave trade.

It should be noted that many persons throughout the newly explored western continent, wherein lies the U.S., were also forcefully converted to Christianity by the Roman Catholic explorers.

But, the point I am making is that Islam is considered by many Black Americans to be their religious roots and that Christianity was forced upon them as slaves. Therefore, they do not view a change from a Christian belief to Islam as a conversion, but rather as a reversion. To them, Islam is the black man's religion, and Christianity is the white man's religion.

Islam had its major establishment in America in the early 1930s when the *Nation of Islam* came into existence. It began to rise to prominence under the leadership of Elijah Muhammad. Who was he?

Daniel Pipes explains:

"He was born Elija Pool in Sandersville, Georgia, in 1897, the seventh of thirteen children. Georgia at that time was an exceedingly racist, violent place and young Elija grew up with searing experiences of white scorn and brutality. The lynching of a friend in 1912 prompted him to flee his parents' house a year later....He fled Georgia for Detroit in 1923, then had the family follow him—the classic story of black migration to the

North. In Detroit, Pool worked in several industrial plants before losing his job and joined a variety of organizations—notably Garbey's Universal Negro Improvement Association (UNIA), a proto-black nationalist movement, and the Black Shriners—but neither of these worked out for him..."

Daniel Pipes, *Militant Islam Reaches America*, (NY: W.W. Norton & Company; 2003): 222-3.

In an effort to improve himself, Poole added an "e" to the end of his name. Then he joined with the Moorish Science Temple of America. There became in league with a person named Wallace D. Fard who had begun a group known as the Allah Temple of Islam-- later to be named the Nation of Islam.

In 1931 Poole's name was changed by Fard to Elijah Karriem. In 1932 it was again changed to Elijah Muhammad. Muhammad's message to those he wished to convert went like this:

"Blacks came into existence 78 trillion years ago and lived an advanced and righteous life through the eons. This came to an end six thousand years ago when a deviant black savant named Mr. Yakub, known as 'the big head scientist,' rebelled against the black gods and created the white race with an eye to destroying the paradise blacks enjoyed. When blacks learned what Mr. Yakub was doing, they exiled him to an island in the Aegean Sea, where he continued his work. Six hundred years later, he had brought the white race into existence, with a mission to reign over blacks for six thousand years. That reign ended in 1914, though a seventy-year period of grace would extend it to 1984; W.D. Fard came to proclaim its end and show blacks how to reclaim their rightful place through the Nation of Islam—something they would definitely do by the year 2000." Ibid. p. 223-4.

In its beginnings the Nation of Islam was only loosely coupled to traditional Islam, but over the years they began to learn and became ever closer to the teachings of Muhammad. When the Nation of Islam began, it was with perhaps only a few dozen people. According to statistics provided by the CIA World Fact Book, and recorded in Wikipedia, the online Encyclopedia, there are 1.35 million Muslims in America as of 2010. 59% of the converts to Islam were from the black communities.

It seems that the black communities haven't bothered to read the history of the slave trade in Africa. It wasn't the West that initially enslaved the blacks; it was primarily Muslim Arabs and black Muslims in Africa who captured the non-Muslim blacks and sold them to the white European and American slave buyers. Slavery wasn't invented by the West; it existed for centuries in the middle-east.

"Islamists espouse deep antagonism toward non-Muslims in general, Jews and Christians in particular. They hate the West both because it is a traditional opponent—the old rival Christendom in a new guise—and because of its huge cultural influence. Some of them have learned to moderate their views so as not to upset western audiences, but this is a thin sugarcoating that should take no one in. Militant Islam is an aggressive global force that explicitly seeks global hegemony just as its fascist and Marxist-Leninist precursors did. In the words of one elected Turkish official, 'We want the whole world to become Muslim, because Islam is the solution to all problems.' Prominent Islamic writers, such as Murad Wilfried Hoffmann, a German convert, have predicted that Islam's ascension to being the dominant world religion is inevitable in this century.

These Islamists cannot merely be laughed off. They must be taken seriously and shown that they cannot impose their totalitarian ways." Ibid. p. 14

"They typically condemn American immorality, consumerism, tolerant social policies, and warm relations with Israel. They talk about 'our society's unrelenting greed' and its neglect for the downtrodden. The prolific Islamist author Maryam Jameelah, a convert from Judaism, in a book titled *Islam versus the West* writes that 'The country which a century ago produced an Abraham Lincoln now has little better to offer the world than Coca-Cola, chewing gum, vulgar songs and filthy pictures" Ibid. p. 129.

What is Chrislam?

Chrislam is a movement that began among the Nigerians. It incorporates both the Bible and the Quran. It has moved to America more as an ideology than a religion. But, it begins with an attempt at brotherhood. Christians are ill informed and horribly naïve concerning the amalgamation.

It usually consists of the Imam reading from the Bible and the Pastor reading from the Quran. How could that be harmful? Perhaps that is what Solomon thought when he first accommodated one of his wives by bringing a 'harmless' object into

Jerusalem's temple.

The goal of Islam is to dominate the religious world. The Islamic fundamentalist view is that it is not a sin to lie to an infidel if it furthers the cause of Islam. That is called *taqiyyah*. To them it is no different than lying to a cow or a dog.

Like the communists/socialists, they will make any deal or enter into any agreement, and break that deal or agreement when it is in the best interest of Islam to do so. Christians need to study the world and not just swallow what the media tells them.

You can live side by side with Islam if you willingly surrender your faith and accept the teachings of Muhammad. You cannot live side by side with Islam, in peace, if you are a Christian. There can be no legitimacy in 'Chrislam.'

Is the Nation of Israel in jeopardy from Islam?

Front Page Magazine on their website:

"When an enemy gives insight into his strategic thinking, it pays to listen. A Hezbollah member of Lebanon's parliament, retired Brigadier-General Walid Sakariya, predicts that Israel will be destroyed by a "Shiite crescent" in a war with hundreds of thousands of deaths. This war, he says, can only commence once two things happen: Iraq is absorbed into Iran's bloc after a U.S. withdrawal and the Syrian regime is saved.

Sakariya says that Iraq is blocking plans to destroy Israel by acting as a "buffer zone." Once U.S. forces completely leave, Iraq will fall to the Iranian-Syrian-Hezbollah axis, permitting Iranian forces to march through its territory. A "Shiite crescent" is created, bringing together over 100 million people in a war against Israel, he explains. He recognizes the high cost of such a conflict, and predicts "hundreds of thousands" of "martyrs" and the use of nuclear weapons by Israel. To Sakariya, the prize of destroying Israel is worth that price. The war hasn't started only because Iran's bloc anticipates more permissible conditions.

However, Sakariya concedes that the plan to destroy Israel requires preserving Syria as a member of the "confrontation" bloc and adding Iraq. Iran has undoubtedly made achieving these objectives its top priority."

"If Syria, as a confrontation country, fails, America and the Zionist enterprise will be victorious he said."
http://frontpagemag.com/2011/08/18/hezbollah-official-destroy-israel-after-u-s-leaves-iraq/).

CONCLUSION

We have examined three major threats to our Christian way of life: Secular Humanism; Governmental Legislation and Court decisions; and Islam. We are very possibly in the last days described by Paul: *"Preach the Word; be prepared in season and out of season; correct, rebuke and encourage—with great patience and careful instruction; for the time will come when men will not put up with sound doctrine. Instead, to suit their own desire, they will gather around them a great number of teachers to say what their itching ears want to hear"* (II Timothy 4:2-3).

If the Church continues to ignore the threats described in this book, we risk losing our youth to humanist philosophies. We will watch as our influence within the government gradually erodes away. We will sit idly by while a vigorous enemy, under a guise of peace, undermines us and surreptitiously gains advantages over us in their effort to eradicate us from the earth.

Throughout the world today, Christians are being persecuted and killed for their faith, and primarily by Muslims. It is a form of genocide where only the Muslims survive and those enslaved by them. Just because it is not happening in the U.S. somehow we believe ourselves to be immune. But, many voices in protest of Muslim extremism have been permanently silenced in Holland, France, Denmark, and Great Britain. Many in Europe are already preparing for a Muslim domination. How long until those who speak out against the threats of Militant Islam will be targeted and silenced in the United States?

Many members of our government, universities, and news media, have been lulled into believing that Islam is a peaceful religion. They have accepted the falsehood that only a minority of radicals have resorted to terrorism in the name of that religion. Such is not the case.

Our government, our colleges and universities, and the news media, need to study: history, the Quran, the Hadith, and all other things pertaining to Islam. It can only be considered a religion, as compared to Judaism, Christianity, Buddhism, etc. in a secondary sense—it is a system of societal jurisprudence first and foremost. They live in peace with "infidels" only when they are powerless to do otherwise. ***The Islamic view of peace is for the entire world to be under the control of Islam, then*** *peace, in their minds, will prevail.*

Is it time for the Militant Church of Jesus Christ to rise up and stand in unity as a phalanx of Christian Soldiers against any threat to the cause of Christ and the intimidation of believers? Have we not polished our boots in the barracks long enough? The "field of battle" is not within the four walls of the First Church of Frigid Air pastored by Dr. Drydust, nor the Church of Unrealistic Promises, pastored by Dr. Makum Feelgood.

We need revival in America. We need a move of the Holy Spirit that will bring Christians back to life and Muslims forward to Christ. The Book of Revelation speaks of those who were killed in the tribulation and those who were beheaded for the name of Christ—it's already happening in parts of the world (Rev. 7:14 & 20:4).

We need an informed clergy, rightly dividing the Word of Truth, and accurately assessing the condition of the world; men or women who can spiritually discern that which is of God, and the Holy Spirit, from that which is not.

"And no wonder, for Satan himself masquerades as an angel of light. It is not surprising, then, if his servants masquerade as servants of righteousness"... (II Corinthians 11:14-15).

Muhammad claims he was visited and given the verses in the Quran by the angel Gabriel. Joseph Smith claims he was visited by an angel that he called Moroni and that he was given verses on golden plates for the Book of Mormon--supposedly directly from God. They each have their own book and they differ. They both claim that their's is a perfect book. Were the angels confused?

The Christian Church was built upon an empowerment by the Holy Spirit to become witnesses to the Gospel of Jesus Christ throughout the world. In most churches the Holy Spirit is a thought, an expression, some kind of ethereal force which is applied in certain situations by Jesus. The Holy Spirit is a person. It is He who is in this world until Jesus comes back. He has lost none of His power—then what happened? It is a question for today's Church to ask, and to which, prayerfully seek an answer.

---The End---

ABOUT THE AUTHOR

Gerald (Jerry) Terrebrood is a 22 year veteran of the U.S. Navy retiring with the rank of LT in 1980. He earned a BA from Central Bible College in 1986, an MA from Assemblies of God Theological Seminary in 1987 and a PhD from Newburgh Theological Seminary in 2012. He pastored three churches, was the Academic Dean at 2 colleges, and the President of two colleges. He retired in February 2006.

www.ingramcontent.com/pod-product-compliance
Lightning Source LLC
Chambersburg PA
CBHW060518030426
42337CB00015B/1939